Building Self-Esteem with Adult Learners

Building Self-Esteem with Adult Learners

DENIS LAWRENCE

P·C·P
Paul Chapman
Publishing Ltd

Paul Chapman Publishing Ltd
A SAGE Publications Company
6 Bonhill Street
London EC2A 4PU

SAGE Publications Inc
2455 Teller Road
Thousand Oaks, California 91320

SAGE Publications India Pvt Ltd
32, M-Block Market
Greater Kailash -I
New Delhi 110 048

British Library Cataloguing in Publication data

A catalogue record for this book is available from the British Library

ISBN 0-7619-5474-0
ISBN 0-7619-5475-9 (pbk)

Library of Congress catalog card number available

Typeset by Dorwyn Ltd, Rowlands Castle, Hants
Printed and bound in Great Britain

Contents

List of figures vii
Foreword ix
Preface xi
Acknowledgements xv
Introduction xvii

1 THE SELF-CONCEPT 1
Self-image 2
Ideal self 3
Self-esteem 4
Summary 7

2 THE STUDENT'S PERSONALITY 9
Basic temperaments 10
Measuring personality traits 12
Origins of low self-esteem 15
Summary 24

3 THE STUDENT WITH SPECIAL EDUCATIONAL
NEEDS 25
Hearing difficulties 26
Visual difficulties 27
General learning difficulties 28
The dyslexic student 29
Summary 32

4 ASSESSING PROGRESS AND MAINTAINING
MOTIVATION 34
Maintaining motivation 35
Formal examinations 39
Summary 40

5   DEVELOPING THE SKILLS   41
    The modelling effect   41
    Acceptance, genuineness and empathy   42
    Becoming sensitive to non-verbal cues   51
    A self-help approach to developing confidence as a tutor   52
    Summary   54

6   THE TUTORING SESSION   55
    The setting   55
    The materials   55
    Meeting the student   56
    Handling the session   59
    Summary   64

7   THE SELF-ESTEEM ENHANCEMENT PROGRAMME   66
    Introduction   66
    Session 1: Introducing the Self-Esteem Enhancement
    Programme to the student   67
    Session 2: Developing spontaneity and self-acceptance   72
    Session 3: Looking the part – body language   75
    Session 4: Being assertive   78
    Session 5: Coping with stress   83
    Session 6: Strengthening the Self   91

8   DEVELOPING A POSITIVE LIFESTYLE   96
    Setting goals   97
    Developing your skills   98
    Becoming an expert   98
    Having fun   99
    Conclusion   100

    Selected bibliography   101
    Index   103

List of figures

Figure 1   The self-concept   1
Figure 2   Maslow's hierarchy of needs   5
Figure 3   Hans Eysenck's Dimensions of Personality   13
Figure 4   IQ distribution   28
Figure 5   Graph of student's progress   38
Figure 6   The structure of the mind   93

Foreword

Dr Denis Lawrence has worked for many years with children and adults who have found difficulty mastering basic literacy skills. He has researched the importance played by confidence and self-esteem in the learning process and, in 1995, he shared that knowledge with tutors and students in Link into Learning, Cornwall County Council's Adult Basic Education programme.

Adults who come to seek help with their basic skills often do so after a lifetime of avoiding situations where they might be seen to fail. They are usually very self-depreciating and nervous. They are lacking in confidence and their self-esteem is very low. This creates a barrier to learning which can be greater than any other factor.

We are grateful to Denis for highlighting the importance of confidence and self-esteem in being able to harness students' learning abilities to improve their skills. We are now developing an Initial Learning Programme for all new students, which concentrates on improving their confidence and self-esteem by reflecting on their learning achievements in the widest sense, giving them an understanding of their own learning strengths and weaknesses. Through this programme we aim to help students to improve their own view of themselves and give them the belief in their own ability to learn which is vital to enable them to retain the skills and knowledge they gain.

The learning opportunities we offer are based on the principle of students taking control of their own learning. Without a belief in their own learning ability and the confidence to take on situations in which there is a risk of failure, this would be impossible.

Janet Anderson
Principal, Link into Learning
Cornwall's Adult Education Basic Skills Service

Preface

When I was a boy we had a plaque upon the kitchen wall in our house which had this motto printed on it in large letters – DEFEAT IS ONLY FOR THOSE WHO ACCEPT IT. This was during the Second World War and my mother used to recite it from time to time, especially when the air-raid sirens used to sound. I doubt very much whether I understood what it meant as I was only a young boy in those days, but I do remember the feeling of security and strength it gave. Life was very different in those war years. My father, like many other fathers, was away in the Armed Forces; there was no TV and usually we played outside on the streets for our entertainment. Mostly we played happily enough, although it was not unusual for our play to be interrupted by the sound of the air-raid siren. I remember well the initial feeling of apprehension as the warning siren sounded and we made our way to the air-raid shelter in the garden. Once we had made the relative safety of the shelter my mother would talk to us reassuringly and the motto on the kitchen wall often cropped up in the conversation. Many years have gone by since those troubled times, but on various occasions since I have found myself reciting this motto, usually in times of stress, and it has always provided me with the same sense of security and optimism I experienced a long time ago whenever it was recited. I commend it to all those students who may from time to time be faced with stress in their lives and may at times doubt their ability to make progress.

The growing interest in self-esteem enhancement

During the winter of 1995 I had occasion to visit an adult education centre in the small Cornish town of St Austell. This centre is much like many others around the country. People meet there regularly for help with their literacy skills provided for them by dedicated tutors, many of whom are volunteers. It was noticed, however, that this centre was unusual. The approach of the tutors was not the usual kind of tutoring. Students were chatting with their tutors and it became clear that the students were not only receiving help with their reading, writing and spelling but were also being valued and given opportunity to talk about themselves. It seemed to me that a more accurate description of what was taking place was not merely 'tutoring' but 'self-esteem enhancement'. Self-esteem was being raised at the same time as improvements in literacy skills were taking place. After discussing this with the tutors, it also became clear that this self-esteem approach was taking place intuitively and with no theoretical base. It occurred to me that their approach could be even more effective if the tutors were given a sound theoretical base for what they were doing and perhaps a more structured programme to raise self-esteem.

Accordingly, two workshops on the topic of Self-Esteem Enhancement were organised at which the principles outlined in this book were discussed together with practical role-playing exercises in raising self-esteem. Following the workshops the tutors agreed to assess the effects of their self-esteem tutoring and students were assessed on standardised measures of reading, spelling, self-esteem and general confidence.

Six months later, they were reassessed on all measures and the results were truly astounding. Dramatic gains had been made on all variables. It had been anticipated that another adult literacy tutored group which had not received the self-esteem workshops would act as a control group. Although this group had agreed to be tested at the outset of the experiment, unfortunately it proved impossible to reassess them for various reasons outside my control. Critics of the method could therefore rightly conclude that without a control group it is not possible to claim that the self-esteem input was entirely responsible for the dramatic rises. However, in the light of my previous research into the effects of self-esteem enhancement with children it would not seem unreasonable to conclude that the particular self-esteem approach adopted by these tutors was indeed the main reason for the dramatic improvements. Further support for this conclusion came from discussing the results with the students themselves, who claimed in no uncertain terms that they felt so much more confident since their sessions. Research in the area of the psychological construct known as self-esteem would certainly support this view.

The self-esteem construct

The self-esteem construct is recognised today to be a major factor in learning outcomes. Research has consistently shown a positive correlation between how people value themselves and the level of their academic attainments. Those who feel confident generally achieve more, while those who lack confidence in themselves achieve less. People tend to behave in terms of how they perceive themselves. Those who believe that they are capable of succeeding are more likely to do so, because a person's image of themselves largely determines what they do. The self-image is a motivator. Moreover, those with high self-esteem not only achieve more but tend also to lead more satisfying lives. The high self-esteem person is more spontaneous in relationships with others and impresses as being more trustworthy. Other people warm to them more quickly as a result so that they have a greater chance of finding satisfaction in their relationships.

The development of high self-esteem, therefore, should be just as valuable a goal for educationists as the development of intellectual skills; and research supports this view.

The research indicates that self-esteem and intellectual attainments are inextricably linked, with both affecting and influencing each other. It is not possible to separate the emotions from the intellect. The person who is over-anxious, for instance, is not able to think as clearly; and the person who has a problem thinking clearly is likely to become anxious about it. A learning programme which does not take this phenomenon into account is not going to function effectively.

Education, of whatever skill, needs to be concerned with the whole person and not just with that part known as the intellect. Although, traditionally, education has not ignored the role of the emotions the focus has been mainly on the negative emotions – questions of control and punishment, particularily with children in schools. In today's educational climate, however, teachers usually appreciate the positive role of emotions and the need to establish rapport with their pupils. It is the emotions associated with the self-concept, however, which still appear relatively neglected. Tutors need to be aware of the need people have for self-esteem. They will become more skilled as tutors once they have appreciated this need and then learned how to organise their tutoring to cater for it.

It is now 20 years since my research into enhancing self-esteem in the classroom, which culminated in a book of the same title, and it is pleasing to note that today many teachers in the primary and secondary sectors of education are putting into practice the results of that research and teaching for the improvement of self-esteem. In the field of further and higher education, however, it seems that the powerful role of the pupil's self-esteem in learning is not always fully appreciated, despite the evidence that self-esteem and attainments complement each other. Although most tutors recognise the importance of establishing good rapport and of maintaining the self-esteem of their students, it is rare for tutors to organise their tutoring sessions systematically so that they are designed for self-esteem enhancement. This book aims to correct that omission and to provide those interested tutors with practical methods of self-esteem enhancement to be used alongside the teaching of the basic literacy skills. If this is done successfully students will not only have improved their literacy skills but will also have become happier people.

Acknowledgements

I wish to offer my thanks and my admiration to all those students and their tutors engaged on adult literacy courses throughout the county of Cornwall. I wish to give a special thanks to those in the Saltash Link into Learning Centre who so willingly continue to gave up their time to talk to me. A particular thanks to the tutors and students on the St Austell Link into Learning course, who agreed to participate in the experiments referred to in the book during which the self-esteem approach to tutoring was outlined.

I am gratefully indebted to my wife, Anne, for her valuable support and encouragement to me while completing the manuscript and also for her valuable suggestions and amendments to the manuscript. Finally, thanks to Marianne Lagrange at Paul Chapman Publishing whose expert guidance and advice throughout the writing of the manuscript has been invaluable.

Introduction

The ability to read is something most of us take for granted as it is a skill we learned a long time ago when at school. For some people, however, reading was something they found difficult to learn when at school and the problem has persisted well into their adult years. The precise number of people who fall into this category is unclear but from official surveys it seems likely that as many as 25 per cent of the population of the English-speaking world have a reading problem of some kind, ranging from not being able to read at all to having a limited level of reading attainment where reading is a slow and laborious process. In addition to a reading problem many of these people have associated difficulties with spelling and writing.

The causes of literacy difficulties have occupied educationalists for decades and from the plethora of research on the topic it is clear that there are a variety of reasons for the problem. Whatever the reasons, the emotional and social consequences of not being able to read and spell properly are distressing. The embarrassment of having to admit to not being able to fill in the simplest form can be the source of acute distress. In addition, living in a largely literate society, such people are isolated from so much that the more literate take for granted and the barriers they can encounter are numerous. Occupational choices are obviously limited, leisure opportunities are restricted, and even a simple visit to the local shop can produce severe problems for those unable to read. For some, the continual pressure of learning to cope with their literacy weakness can result in enormous stress. So what began a long time ago in school as an educational problem gradually becomes a social and emotional problem. With regular failure in a skill that society values, people eventually lose confidence in themselves generally. It should come as no surprise to discover that there is an association between literacy skills and self-esteem. People who have low attainments in literacy usually have lower self-esteem than the rest of us.

It is interesting to note that people who have low self-esteem react to this problem in different ways according to their basic temperament. The more introverted will tend to react by withdrawing from social contacts and be nervous and timid. The more extraverted in temperament will kick back at a world they perceive as being unfair and may become either aggressive or boastful and arrogant.

It is also interesting that the research into self-esteem shows that people tend to behave according to how they perceive themselves. So those who perceive themselves as poor readers, for example, are not so likely to pick up a book or to visit a library. This example shows how a person's self-image acts as a motivator, determining experiences. This is why it is so important for tutors to help students change their self-image and begin to see themselves more positively. Without a change in their perception of themselves, even if students learn to read they are not likely to bother to practise their new-found skills outside the tutoring session. Their habit of viewing themselves as poor readers will continue. The main aim of this book is to demonstrate to tutors how they can help students change this negative perception of themselves to more a positive one and so enhance their self-esteem.

It is probably true that tutors working in the field of adult literacy are intuitively aware of the importance of helping students with their self-esteem. Very few tutors, however, are aware of the various strategies available that have been designed specifically to enhance self-esteem, or have a knowledge of self-esteem theory. A further aim of the book is to provide tutors with an opportunity to refine their own, often intuitive approach to self-esteem enhancement by practising these strategies (and in so doing they will enhance their own self-esteem also).

The first chapters aim to provide tutors with an understanding of students' psychological needs and also to give tutors guidance on developing specific teaching skills in themselves conducive to self-esteem enhancement. Chapter 1 consists of a description of self-concept theory and illustrates how this concept is related to achievement. Chapter 2 helps tutors understand the individual differences encountered among students and also the factors that contribute to the development of self-esteem. This section also illustrates the psychology of individual differences in temperament and the origins of these. Chapter 3 discusses the development of self-esteem in the student with special educational needs. Ways of maintaining motivation and also how to monitor and record the progress of students without reducing their self-esteem are discussed in Chapter 4. Chapter 5 focuses on developing skills in the tutor that contribute to the enhancement of self-esteem in their students. It draws on the relevant research illustrating how the tutor should try to develop particular qualities in themselves. A selection of exercises and activities is presented for this purpose. Chapter 6 focuses on organising the tutoring session within a self-esteem enhancing framework. It also discusses some common problems in the classroom.

The final chapter of the book consists of the Self-Esteem Enhancement Programme with exercises and strategies for developing self-esteem in students. The Programme, which in its entirety consists of six session, is presented in individual sessions. A selection of activities on a specific theme is presented in each session. It may not always be necessary for students to follow the whole programme. Sometimes only part of the programme may be used, as for example for a student who appears to be generally well adjusted but seems to need to be more assertive. In this case only the exercises on developing assertion would be given as outlined in Session 4. Each session has independent merit and so can be used selectively in this way or in combination with other sessions as deemed necessary. The sessions should be regarded as resources to be used as and when the tutor deems necessary, with some of the activities given as 'homework' and for discussion at the next meeting. The final chapter in the book suggests ways of developing a positive lifestyle and should be of value to both students and tutors.

It is hoped that *Building Self-Esteem with Adult Learners* will prove useful both for tutors employed in colleges of further education, teaching basic literacy courses, and also for volunteer tutors engaged in adult literacy programmes. Whether the students have only recently left school, or whether they are adults with long-standing literacy difficulties, they will all have in common the need for self-esteem enhancement.

Chapter 1

The self-concept

The main aim of the book is to help tutors develop self-esteem in their students. However, in order to be able to practise the principles of self-esteem enhancement it is important to be aware of the theoretical framework underlying the various exercises and strategies outlined later in the book. Our starting point is the term **self-concept**. This is one of those terms in psychology which has come to be used in everyday life and as a result is often used to mean many different things. For our purposes the self-concept of a person is best defined as an awareness of the mental and physical attributes that make up a person, together with their feelings about their attributes. As such it is an 'umbrella' term beneath which lie the concepts of **self-image, ideal self** and **self-esteem**. This is depicted in Figure 1.

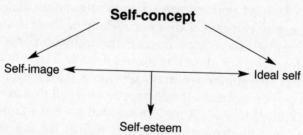

Figure 1   The self-concept

The figure also illustrates how a person's self-esteem is dependent on the relationship between their *self-image* and their ideal self. These terms are defined, and their relationships to each other and to self-esteem explained, in the following sections.

Self-image

This is the image we have of ourselves. If asked the question 'Who are you?' people would normally list their mental and their physical characteristics which together make up their unique person. The self-image begins to be formed shortly after birth. At first it is merely a physical image as the baby gradually realises that its limbs are part of itself. This can be amusing for the parents as the baby accidently bites its own foot. Gradually, the self-image is enlarged as the baby comes into contact with the environment. Parents normally begin this process of development of the self-image by communicating the kind of person the baby is, e.g. 'You are beautiful!' The process continues throughout babyhood and into childhood. Teachers continue the process saying things like, 'You are clever' (or the opposite!). 'You are big, come to the front.' Through encounters with other people, children learn many more things about themselves such as, they can or cannot run fast, read well, are popular, etc. Both mental and physical characteristics are learned as the child bounces off the environment in this way. As the process continues during the schools years children soon begin to learn whether they are good at academic things, and particularly at literacy tasks.

By adulthood most of us have a pretty good idea of the kind of people we are and the kind of skills and abilities we have. The more experiences we have the richer will be our self-image. We will have learned that we are competent in some areas of our lives but not so competent in others. Many of these impressions of ourselves will have been learned through comparisons with others. However, not all of our impressions will be wholly accurate so that sometimes we may develop a false notion of ourselves in certain respects. If this happens we call this developing a 'distorted self-image'. It may mean that we have come to believe we have inadequacies when in reality we are relatively competent. For instance, the person of average ability may believe they are below average simply because the people whom they meet regularly are all well above average. The people they have been comparing themselves with were probably a small sample of the general population and not representative of the population as a whole.

But adults with literacy difficulties generally perceive themselves fairly accurately as they would normally have had plenty of experience trying to cope in a society which expects people to be literate. During school years they would have had ample opportunities to compare themselves with their peers. As schools are primarily places of academic learning, children with literacy difficulties are continually being challenged by their difficulties. Usually by the time they are adults they will have learned ways of hiding their limitations, or at least they will have learned to avoid those situations in which they may have to reveal their inadequacies. They may, for instance, always ensure that a relative or a friend fills in forms for them. Their self-images, having been formed largely in childhood, will continue to motivate them as adults and so they will try to avoid what they perceive as potentially inferiority-inducing situations. Their self-images have told them that they are not able to perform as well as most other people and they will not want to be seen failing. The need to preserve self-esteem is a very powerful psychological need in us all.

Ideal self

As awareness develops in a child and their self-image begins to be formed, they begin to be aware that the adults around them reward certain kinds of behaviour in them. For instance, amongst the early social behaviour, most children learn that saying 'Thank you' is rewarded. And so the ideal self begins to form as they learn that there are standards of behaviour and levels of achievement which the adults value. They learn that adults like them to be clean and tidy, to be clever in school and to be good at sports. In other words, they are learning that there are socially desirable things which are valued in the kind of society in which they live and it is these values which together form the ideal self. As they develop, these values of society are unconsciously followed. By the adult stage the values of society generally have become their own values, although some of them may have been questioned along the way, and may even have been rejected.

In summary, the ideal self is a collection of ideal values, standards of behaviour and abilities to which a person aspires. Amongst these normally would be the ability to read, write and spell like most other people. Social skills are also part of the ideal self of most people, so being able to get on with other people is usually part of the ideal self.

Self-esteem

This is the aspect of the self-concept which concerns us in practice and which is the main subject of this book. It can be defined theoretically as a person's evaluation of the discrepancy between their self-image and their ideal self. As described above, most adults have a fairly good idea of the kind of person they are and also of the kind of person they would like to be. Generally, we all have room for improvement in this respect although there are some people who are reluctant and even resistant to facing up to this fact. On the whole, however, people are well aware that there is likely to be some degree of discrepancy between their self-image (what they are) and their ideal self (what they would like to be). This is normal and the healthy person is motivated by this discrepancy to improve and so move closer to the ideal self. The question is – how much does the person care that they have not yet reached their ideal? This will depend largely on how far the characteristics in question are valued by those whose opinions we care about. For instance, most adults will care very much about not being able to read, whereas not being able to play golf will not be such an issue. However, even the latter could be a source of distress to somebody who regularly moves in golf circles where all their acquaintances value that sport.

When people care deeply about not reaching their ideal, eventually they feel failures and begin to dislike themselves. Their feelings of failure in one important area have generalised to the whole personality. This is what is usually meant by low self-esteem. In practice, self-esteem can be defined as **confidence** and as such it has two aspects:

- confidence in personality, and
- confidence in abilities.

We say that people who have low self-esteem lack confidence in themselves so that they are reluctant to take risks either personally or in the learning of a new skill, e.g. reading. They will be so aware of their inadequacies, both as people and in their skills, that they will tend to avoid situations which they perceive as likely to cause them further unpleasant feelings.

The need for self-esteem

It is probably true to say that the need for self-esteem is the most important need we have in our kind of society. Traditional psychology textbooks will list self-preservation, hunger, thirst and sex as being amongst the most important needs but in our kind of society these needs are relatively easily satisfied for most of us. The need to be valued and to be liked is not always so easily satisfied and yet it is a need we all possess. Everywhere people seem to be striving to maintain their self-esteem, whether between workers and management in industry, between countries, between parents and children, or between teachers and children. Countless numbers of people can be seen at every level in society desperately trying to compensate for feelings of inadequacy, real or imaginary.

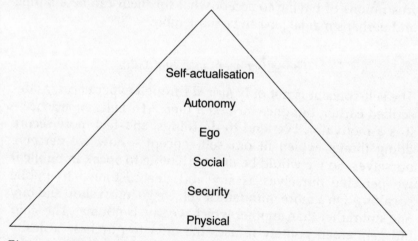

Figure 2 Maslow's hierarchy of needs

Some years ago the eminent psychologist, Abraham Maslow, postulated a heirarchy of needs in humans. This is presented in Figure 2, illustrating how personal needs – consisting of physiological needs – at the bottom of the heirarchy, have to be satisfied first before the more intellectual and social needs at the top of the heirarchy. The implication is that people cannot expect to be concerned with satisfying their social needs such as self-esteem unless their basic physiological needs are satisfied first. This may have to be taken into account by tutors if, for instance, students are economically disadvantaged. They may have difficulty in affording the cost of course books once basic costs for food and bus fares have been met. For most students with problems of literacy, however, their basic needs are being satisfied and their need for self-esteem is much more in evidence. This need remains unsatisfied as they continually encounter other people who do not have their problems.

The sad fact is that such people often become totally accepting of their feelings of inadequacy. They see themselves as inadequate and have decided that they are not as valuable as other people. As a result they usually accept second best in life; indeed without the skill of literacy they inevitably find themselves in jobs which are less demanding. This is probably not so much a problem in cases where the person concerned is not academically inclined, but where the person is of a higher intellect the frustrations of having to accept what for them can be a boring and perhaps menial job can be intolerable.

The self-concept as a motivator

The self-concept is not only *formed* through experiences, as described earlier, but once formed it then *determines* experience – it is a motivator. We tend to do things, and feel more secure doing things, which fit our self-concept – how we perceive ourselves. So we would be uneasy having to speak in public if we perceive ourselves as shy and unaccustomed to public speaking. On a more mundane level, we go into a shop and buy one suit rather than another which we say 'Is not me'. The staid old gentleman politely refuses the offer to purchase a flashy new open-top sports car and goes instead for the shiny saloon with, 'I think the saloon is more me'. The person who cannot read is not likely to go into a library or to buy a daily newspaper. We all tend to behave according to how we perceive ourselves. This is why it is so important for tutors to understand the nature of each student's self-concept. Without first seeing themselves as possible good readers the motivation will not be there. Students will not make permanent progress unless tutors take into account the need to help them change their self-concepts as well as teaching them new skills. Without a change in how they perceive themselves they will go through the motions of learning but they will not retain the material in the long term. Once they begin to feel different they are more likely to practise their new-found skills.

Most tutoring takes place once a week and it is then up to the student to practise at home the skills learned in their weekly session. At first, most students are likely to have low self-esteem so their motivation to practise will be low and they will be content to wait until the next session before making any more effort to learn. Many of them will have learned from past experience that the teacher does the work! This is another reason why it is essential that tutors help these students change their self-concepts.

Following the tutoring/self-esteem enhancement approach, progress will be quicker as students will not only leave the sessions with improved skills but also with a modified self-concept. With self-esteem enhancement they will gradually begin to perceive themselves in a more positive light and be more motivated to learn. Consequently, not only are they likely to be better motivated to practise outside the tutoring sessions but as motivation is stronger the material learned will be remembered longer.

Summary

- Self-concept is an 'umbrella' term comprising self-image, ideal self and self-esteem.
- Self-image is an awareness of a collection of mental and physical characteristics.
- Ideal self is an awareness of ideal characteristics or levels of aspiration.
- Self-esteem is the evaluation of the discrepancy between self-image and ideal self.
- Low self-esteem in literacy skills generalises to the whole personality.
- Self-concept is a motivator – it can determine behaviour.

Further reading

Burns, R. B. (1979) *The Self-concept*. London: Longman.

Burns, R. B. (1982) *Self-concept Development and Education*. London: Holt-Rhinehart.

Lawrence, D. (1987) *Enhancing Self-esteem in the Classroom*. London: Paul Chapman.

Chapter 2

The student's personality

One of the first goals for the tutor should be to try to understand the student's personality – what makes the student tick. This means a little more than just getting to know the student. It means also learning a little about what makes for individual differences in people.

Social psychologists have shown us how we are all different in some ways but also that we are all alike in other ways. Students with literacy problems all have different personalities. Some are extraverted and so like working in a group. Some are introverted and prefer to work in a one-to-one situation. Some are shy and some are not. However, they are all the same in one sense. All of them are returning to study after years of failure in a skill which society values highly and as a result are likely to show many of the symptoms of low self-esteem. They will be somewhat apprehensive and they may be insecure about asking for help. An understanding of each student's personality will help tutors in the best aproach to their teaching. It will help them also to understand behaviour in their students which can sometimes be bewildering but which may be merely an expression of underlying inferiority feelings. A knowledge of the student's personality and what motivates them is useful to the tutor in the establishment of the necessary self-esteem enhancing relationship. It is the quality of this relationship that is the key to successful self-esteem enhancement. Without a good student–tutor relationship it is unlikely that the exercises and the activities outlined in Chapter 7 of the book will make much difference.

Basic temperaments

All students are different. That may seem obvious enough, but it is worth emphasising this fact as we all have a tendency at times to group people in categories and to treat them as if they are all the same. This is especially true in teaching, where it is often more economic to teach large groups of people at once. In so doing it is easy to forget that the grouping of students is more likely to be based on adminstrative and economic considerations rather than on individual educational need.

A question often asked is how much of individual differences between people is due to heredity and how much is due to environment. Much research has been done on this question over the years and the conclusion is that differences in personality are due both to the effects of different environmental influences *and* inherited characteristics. In other words we are a combination of heredity and environment. The relative contributions of heredity and environment have occupied research workers for decades but the evidence is that we all have a basic inherited temperament and other personality characteristics are environmentally determined.

Many years ago Carl Jung made the observation that people seemed to differ along one important dimension. He called this the introvert/extravert dimension. Some people appeared to prefer quiet pursuits and were generally quieter people than others. These he called the introverts. Another sort of person seemed to prefer noisier pursuits and was usually seen to be the 'life and soul of the party'. These people he called the extraverts. Although some people seemed to have a predisposition to be one or the other, most people seemed to be a mixture of the two. Since that time the work of psychologists like Eysenck and Cattell have shown how it is possible to measure these characteristics using questionnaires. Moreover, they have shown how extraverts become bored more quickly than introverts and seem to work best in short bursts. Introverts work best in longer periods and do not seem to need the continual variety that extraverts appear to demand.

In addition to this dimension of personality, a second dimension has been identified referred to as 'emotionality'. Some people seem always to be highly emotional and perhaps oversensitive whilst another group seems always to be somewhat placid and lacking in emotional expression. We are all capable of experiencing emotions – humans are emotional creatures; however, some are more emotional than others. Some people when happy are elated and when unhappy are in the depths of depression. They always seem to be worrying about something and tend to take offence easily; they are considered oversensitive. At the other end of the scale there are those people who seem hardly ever to be emotional or unduly upset. They take life as it comes, although sometimes they can be accused of being insensitive. As with the introvert/extravert dimension, most people are in the middle with an average amount of emotionality.

It seems from the research evidence that these two dimensions of personality appear shortly after birth and, because there appears to be a physiological basis for them, remain relatively unchanged throughout life. A knowledge of these personality traits in their students will help tutors understand them better. For instance, it seems that people get on more easily with those of a similar personality type, so obviously if the tutor is an extravert and the student is an introvert there is likely to be a personality clash. They will find that they do not easily understand each other and the relationship will be uneasy. In the case of the introvert it helps a tutor to know that their student's apparently withdrawn behaviour is no more than a natural personality characteristic and is not a personal reaction to them. Also it is useful to know that the introvert can safely be given a longer task than the extravert as their boredom threshold is higher.

There is another important reason for knowing where a student lies on the introvert/extravert dimension. People tend to react to frustration in terms of their basic temperament. An extravert would react to low self-esteem in an extraverted fashion, i.e. outwardly, possibly with a show of bravado. The extraverted student can sometimes be heard declaring boldly 'I don't care that I can't read!' or making some other outrageous comment, kicking back at the world, blaming it for their frustration. An introvert, on the other hand, would react inwardly, possibly by timid, withdrawn behaviour, perhaps being unwilling to tackle new material for fear of further humiliations.

It is equally useful for the tutor to understand the degree of emotionality in their student. The highly emotional student is likely to become more more upset at failures and be more sensitive to praise, for instance. Also, the emotional student may benefit from relaxation techniques before beginning a session to help lower their degree of emotionality as it is known that too much emotion interferes with clear thinking. Techniques for this are outlined in the self-esteem module later in the book.

It is important to emphasise that these dimension of personality are not necessarily related to mental ill health. In other words, people can be at either extreme of the dimensions and be perfectly healthy and well adjusted. However, a person at either of the extremes on both dimensions is going to be more at risk of developing problems. For instance, a person who is highly emotional and is also highly extraverted is not going to find it easy to work for long periods alone. Their extraversion will mean they will become bored quickly, missing the stimulation of other people's company, and their high emotionality will mean that they are likely to become bad tempered about it. Research into this kind of temperament supports this view. By the same token, a person who is highly introverted and also highly emotional is not going to find it easy working in the company of other people. After a while, their introversion will cause the company of others to irritate them and their emotionality will also cause them to become bad tempered at this frustration. This relationship between introversion/extraversion and emotionality is depicted in Figure 3. Each star in the figure represents a person's score on a questionnaire assessing the two dimensions. It can be seen that most people congregate around the middle of the diagram and so are a bit of each, whilst a minority are at the ends of each continuum.

Measuring personality traits

The best way to learn where students are on these two dimensions of introversion/extraversion and emotionality is to get to know them personally. Once tutors have been able to establish a close and empathic relationship with them they will have a good idea whether their students are over-, or under-emotional;

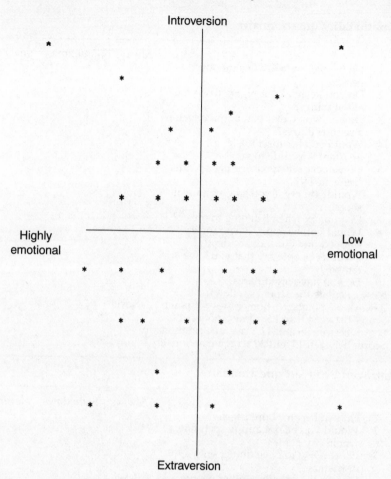

Figure 3   Hans Eysenck's Dimensions of Personality

whether they are introverted or extraverted or, more usually, perhaps, in the middle on these dimensions. However, it is possible to confirm or perhaps reject judgements made on this ad hoc basis by asking students to complete questionnaires. Shortened versions of these questionnaires are presented here in case some students show interest in an assessment. As with all questionnaires, especially shortened ones, the results should be interpreted broadly and with caution. Even if tutors do not wish to use them, the questionnaires do serve the purpose of illustrating further the particular characteristics of introversion/ extraversion and emotionality.

Emotionality questionnaire

		Always	Sometimes	Never

1. Do people say you are a moody person?
2. Do you lie awake at nights worrying about things?
3. Do you worry that you might develop a serious illness?
4. Would you be upset if a shop assistant was rude to you?
5. Do you cry when witnessing a tender scene on TV?
6. Would you cry if you saw an animal shot?
7. Do you cry when listening to music?
8. Would you be angry if a stranger stepped on your foot accidently?
9. Do other people say that you have a temper?
10. Do you have nightmares?

Now calculate the score as follows:
Always = 2 points   Sometimes = 1 point   Never = 0
Scores between 0 and 5 = low emotionality
Scores between 6 and 12 = average emotionality.
Scores between 13 and 20 = high emotionality

Introvert/extravert questionnaire

		Always	Sometimes	Never

1. Do you become bored easily?
2. Would you be unhapppy spending a whole day alone?
3. Do you like to have dinner with a lot of friends?
4. Do you like to talk to other people while shopping?
5. Do you like lively parties?
6. Do you like to go on holiday with lots of people?
7. Do you speak first when meeting people?
8. Would you enjoy talking to a large group?
9. Would you prefer visiting a shop rather than ordering goods by phone?
10. Do you try to vary the kind of clothes you wear?

Now calculate the extravert/introvert score as follows:
Always = 2 points   Sometimes = 1 point   Never = 0
Scores between 0 and 5 = markedly introverted
Scores between 6 and 15 = average (i.e. like most people)
Scores between 16 and 20 = markedly extraverted

Origins of low self-esteem

Students usually have no problem in talking to the tutor about their literacy difficulties. Once they have learned to trust their tutor they will often bring up other problems of a more personal nature. This is not to suggest that tutors become counsellors, but they should be prepared to listen to students who may wish to confide in them. The ability to listen effectively is a skilled process and this topic is developed further in Chapter 5. On another level, it often helps us to understand people better when we know the origins of their difficulties.

Whilst the majority of students are likely to have low self-esteem as a result of feeling inadequate over not being able to read, write or spell like most others, they may in addition have low self-esteem as a result of other experiences, probably beginning in childhood. There will be countless opportunities for the tutor to begin the process of enhancing self-esteem once they know the origins of these. For instance, knowing that a student has had strong feelings of inadequacy since childhood over their physical appearance would allow the tutor to focus positively on valuing the student in this direction as well as in relation to progress in literacy.

Emotional deprivation

Under the normal process of development, we learn from our parents that we are loveable and there is a gradual dawning that this seems to depend largely on how we behave. Some luckless children, however, cannot win no matter how they behave. They may have parents who are unable or unwilling to show consistent love, usually because of their own unresolved problems. So such children learn quite early in life that they are not necessarily loveable. As a result they begin to feel guilty about the kind of people they are and eventually begin to dislike themselves. At this stage in development children usually believe their parents' valuation of them. This is what we call developing low self-esteem. The unloved child eventually becomes the unloved adult. Indeed, many adults are unconsiously seeking desperately the love they were denied as children. If, in addition to early emotional deprivation, they later develop literacy problems it is not surprising that they have extremely low self-esteem as adults.

Unassertive behaviour

Low self-esteem people usually lack assertion. The manner in which this lack of assertion is demonstrated, however, varies according to the individual temperament of the student as discussed previously. In the case of the more extraverted their unassertive behaviour is likely to be expressed aggressively as they attempt to compensate for their feelings of inadequacy – the 'little man with the big voice' syndrome as it is often called. We sometimes say also that a person showing this kind of behaviour has an 'inferiority complex'. In the case of the more introverted, their unassertive behaviour is more likely to be manifested in timidity and perhaps in silently aggressive ways, like remaining passive when expected to react. In both cases it helps to understand that their behaviour is a means of expressing the frustrations of low self-esteem.

As with low self-esteem, unassertive behaviour is learned and usually has its origins in early childhood. The process of socialisation whereby children learn the skills of communicating with others and how to co-operate with them begins very early in life. Most children learn at a young age that it is more satisfying and safer to adopt the standards and values of the adults around them – they learn that they receive approval for good behaviour and punishments for bad behaviour. Children also model themselves on those adults nearest to them and so tend to behave like them. As they go through the various stages of childhood they continue to be influenced in this way and so their conscience is formed. Then they behave in the ways they have learned, even in the absence of their parents, as it just 'feels right'. In the normal process a correct balance between rewards and punishments will be achieved until eventually parents rely less on punishments and more on rewards. These rewards generally take the form in the early years of love from the parents and even in many cases more material things. Not many parents will have resisted the temptation of promising their children a lolly if they behave nicely. As the child moves towards adolescence the system of rewards and punishments should give way to discussion and negotiation, with the child having a say when problems of conflict occur. In this way, children learn that they can express their needs without punishment or fear and later as adults they are more likely to resolve disagreements with others through the same process of negotiation rather than through aggression.

Unfortunately not all children have this kind of upbringing. They may for instance have parents who rely totally on punishments to socialise their children. Under these circumstances they will tend to grow up either as over-aggressive or unduly passive depending again on whether they are by temperament extraverts or introverts. Both are an indication of lack of confidence, or low self-esteem. These people have learned somewhere along the line that some situations cause them to feel anger and as they are unsure of themselves they often either say 'the wrong thing' or say nothing at all. Some learn simply to avoid situations which tend to make them feel angry; they have discovered that it is safer to behave that way. These are the people who would 'rather not get involved'. They sit on the fence when it comes to having to give an opinion. There are different degrees of this kind of behaviour but many people like this find it very stressful to have to commit themselves in public. Another manifestion of unassertive behaviour is the person who says they do not want to commit themselves to an opinion because they do not want to upset somebody. These people often score highly on the emotionality scale. The irony is that trying hard not upset somebody usually results in an even more undesirable reaction – a reputation for being indecisive is acquired and these people are often treated with scorn and mistrusted. If you do not say what you really mean and try to hide what you think, you often end up having to lie and this is communicated through your body language. Your voice tone and facial expressions usually give you away.

The person commonly described as 'shy' is an example of another kind of unassertive behaviour. This person will also tend to avoid situations which past experience has taught them are likely to be unpleasant. However, unlike the previous example, other people are usually more charitable when meeting this kind of unassertive behaviour, although it can be irritating. It is certainly unpleasant for the person who is shy, particularily as shyness is often accompanied by reddening of the skin – blushing. Again, the origins of shyness are usually found in early childhood.

Distorted self-image

Some people have a totally unrealistic image of themselves and are continually surprised when others perceive them in a different way. We say they have a 'distorted self-image'. For instance, some students do not fully appreciate how far behind others they may be in literacy standards and are continually surprised when the tutor points out their deficiencies.

As discussed earlier, our image of ourselves begins to be formed in early childhood as we come into contact with others and then 'bounce off the environment' in general. Parents and other significant people in our lives influence how we see ourselves. We learn from them whether we are loveable, valued people, or the opposite. Sometimes as we grow older many of us begin to realise that this image given to us by other people was not altogether an accurate one. However, such is the power of early conditioning that many of us never wholly perceive our 'true selves'. This would not matter if we lived alone, but as humans are social creatures we do come into contact with others, eventually. I was once asked to see a child professionally for behaviour problems in school and the teacher said that he had been 'spoiled' at home. He would arrive at school and demand attention believing he was entitled to be first in all activities. His parents had indeed given him this image of seeing himself as very special and privileged. Consequently it came as a shock to discover that he had to share the toys and that other children's needs were equally important.

Most of these children eventually learn their 'real image' but there are those who never overcome their early experiences and go through life forever wondering why others treat them harshly. Often they will decide that relationships are too stressful to persist with so they try to avoid them altogether. They either remain with their 'distorted image' and resent other people for what they regard as misunderstanding them, or else they come to accept that they are very different from others and feel guilty about it. Feelings of failure arise and soon they have low self-esteem and lack confidence in all situations. The student with a distorted self-image is particularly difficult to teach. This is why it is imperative that the tutor gains the student's confidence and is able to establish good rapport before attempting to help the student gain a realistic self-image.

Confronting this kind of student with their inadequacies before gaining their confidence would only result in denial from the student, and possibly resentment, making it difficult thereafter to develop good rapport.

Real differences

There is another kind of person who may have a problem with their self-image but this time the problem is not one of a distorted self-image. Instead, it is one which they cannot accept easily. Their self-image is not distorted; they have a realistic image all right but the image of themselves is not one they like. It is a reality in life that everybody is different in some ways, both mentally and physically. Unfortunately, some people find the differences so great as to be hard to tolerate and a source of great distress. An obvious example is a physical deformity, but it could just as easily be a personality characteristic like shyness. Unless they are able to come to terms with their problem these people always show a lack of confidence in themselves.

Coming to terms with these feelings of being different is not easy when so often they cause negative reactions in other people. It is unfortunate, but it is a fact that people who are different will always invite the curiosity of others, at least, and sometimes their negative reactions as well. Moreover, we all tend to make judgements about people on the slenderest of evidence. On first meeting somebody we react first to *what they look like*, then to *what they sound like*, and only last to *what they say*. Moreover, first impressions tend to stick. So if a person we meet for the first time is dressed strangely and speaks differently from ourselves we are inclined to treat them with suspicion. It does not matter that they may have offered a friendly greeting. We know nothing about their personality yet we have made a judgement about them simply on superficial appearance. In this case we are responsible for distorting the person's self-image and they are probably surprised at our suspicious reaction to what was meant to be a friendly greeting.

There always will be individual differences between people. Personality is unique. Even between identical twins there are subtle observable differences. This is because even in the same family nobody occupies the same life space as another. Each of our environments are uniquely experienced. Unfortunately, the differences between some people are quite marked so that they appear to have nothing in common with each other at all. It seems to be a human foible to be wary of those whom we perceive as very different from ourselves. This is why minority groups throughout history have been seen to suffer.

A person with an obvious physical deformity soon meets uneasy reactions from others and is made to feel different. So much pain can be felt that they quickly lose confidence and in future try to avoid contact with others. This is not meant to imply that all those people with a physical deformity lack confidence. Many have been fortunate to have had contact with people who are understanding, or in many cases they have learned how to cope with the ignorant reactions shown by some people.

There are other marked differences between people which are not so obvious as a physical deformity but which can also lead to social isolation. Some people, for instance, have a voice or accent which is very different from those they regularly meet. They can soon become very self-conscious if their contacts keep referring to their voice or accent and before long they lack confidence in themselves. Some sociologists have suggested that the dislike of non-standard English in Britain owes its origin to the land-owning aristocracy's need to emphasise their difference from the rest. It is thought that they deliberately adopted a different way of speaking in order to foster their imagined superiority.

It is not only differences in accent, of course, which can cause friction in society. Differences of race, creed, and colour for generations have contributed to social disharmony and in several notable instances in history they have even contributed to outright war. It could be argued that the one characteristic of a civilised society is its tolerance of individual differences.

Life events

We are all at risk of experiencing trauma in our lives which can cause us to lose confidence in ourselves. Often setbacks are only temporary but sometimes events occur of such severity that it takes years for people to regain their former confidence. Under this heading could come a bereavement, a divorce, a business failure, sudden unemployment, or a forced change of abode. Each of these could be a source of considerable stress to some people during which confidence is temporarily lost. If, on top of these events, a person is also having to cope with limited literacy skills, self-esteem falls even further.

Low ego-strength

There are some people who seem quite unable to face up to the slightest frustration or hardship in life which others seem to take in their stride. What distinguishes these two groups? Once again the origins of these differences are likely to be found in their early childhood experiences. Those who never had demands placed on them, for instance, never had practice in having to cope on their own. If parents have always done things for their children it becomes natural for the children to sit back without needing to make any effort to achieve things. Later in life they tend to give in quickly if confronted with a difficult task. This could apply as much to the person who is finding a mountain harder to climb than anticipated as to the person who finds that addressing a group of people is more difficult than anticipated. Both would be inclined to give in rather than stick at the task. The avoidance of potentially threatening situations then becomes a habit for this kind of person as they eventually lack confidence in the face of any kind of new challenge. The challenge for the tutor is to be able to give emotional support and encouragement to this kind of student through demonstrating to them that they are capable of succeeding.

Ego-defence mechanisms

The psychoanalytical school of psychology has had its critics over the years but there are some insights from this approach that can be helpful in our understanding of people. Notable amongst these are the 'ego-defence mechanisms'. These are the strategies which people often use in everyday life in their efforts to cope with threats to their self-esteem. It helps for tutors to be familiar with the most common of these and the way they tend to be expressed.

Denial

This is the term given to the process of refusing to accept a deficiency. The student with a literacy problem often finds it too painful to accept. Obviously those who have decided to accept help of their own volition are not denying it, but some people come for help under pressure to attend from somebody else, often a friend or relative. This kind of student is likely to appear somewhat blasé and even patronising of other students, and as a result is not easy to teach. They will only begin to accept that they have a problem when they can trust the tutor and it is rare for this to happen in the first interview. Tutors should be prepared, therefore, for this kind of student and not take personally any off-hand behaviour which may even seem to be arrogant. The essential first task for the tutor is to establish a close relationship with the student, obviously as quickly as possible. Once this has been done the student will have more confidence in the tutor and the process of helping the student develop a more realistic self-image can begin. One obvious way of starting this process is to administer a standardised test of attainment so that the student can see how they compare with other people of their age.

Belittling and blaming others

This is a sure way of protecting self-esteem in the face of failure. If a student can blame the tutor for their problems they are absolved from feeling guilty about thier own performance. This is fairly common where students have missed much of their schooling because of behaviour problems and perhaps have even been excluded as a result. Even amongst those who are highly motivated and have accepted their deficiencies blame can be attached to the tutor for their slow progress. Most students will reach a learning 'plateau' when they seem to be making no further progress. Ironically, it is usually those who have made quick initial progress who tend to do this. This is a well-researched phenomenon in educational psychology and is thought to be a time of natural consolidation of the learning. However, students of low self-esteem can be very sensitive to their rate of progress and will quickly demand a reason for any slowing down. It seems to be a natural tendency for some to seek the cause of it in the tutor as they know that they themselves are still keen to learn. If this happens it is important that tutors explain to their students that this is a normal process of learning and that all students go through the plateau at some stage when it seems that no progress is being made. This happens to people no matter what they are learning.

Rationalisation

This is another example of face-saving but the difference between this and the other ego-defence mechanisms is that this one is thought to be an unconscious process. People who 'rationalise' their difficulties really do believe their face-saving explanation is genuine. To 'rationalise' is to give a face-saving reason as an explanation for a deficiency rather than having to accept it. This is something we are all capable of experiencing at some time or another. An example of this would be the student who asserts that they are unable to study for long periods because they tire easily, when in actual fact they are finding the work boring. Whenever a student gives an excuse for not studying, or for not having done expected homework, it raises the possibility of rationalisation. When this happens the aim should be to help the student take responsibility for their behaviour and accept their difficulties. It requires a great deal of sensitivity on the part of the tutor to be able to do this without attacking the student's self-esteem. The tutor should gently try to point out how their story cannot possibly be accurate. Again, it can only be done when a trusting relationship has been established.

Compensation

This is also an unconscious way of dealing with threats to the self. An example would be the student who decides that as he cannot shine in literacy skills he is determined to excel in something else, tennis perhaps. Unfortunately, with low self-esteem there is a tendency to overcompensate for the deficiency. One example of this would be the person who is self-conscious over being small and so tends to swagger and to throw their weight around, to the irritation of everybody else. These people try so hard to hide their deficiency that they go overboard in the opposite direction. If tutors come across this kind of behaviour they need to be aware that the student is more than likely trying to preserve their self-esteem.

To conclude this chapter on understanding the students' personality, it is worth emphasising that knowledge of personality characteristics, together with some insight into the reasons for behaviour, always helps in understanding differences in personality. Differences between people are inevitable and are interesting. If tutors find the behaviour of some students irritating, it is on those occasions particularly that the tutor should try to understand the student by looking beneath the outward behaviour in order to seek the origins of it. More often than not, the student engaged on a literacy course will be a lonely, isolated person with strong feelings of inadequacy, no matter how they may appear on the surface. The next chapter will take the understanding of individual differences in students further by focusing on specific educational needs.

Summary

- There are two basic temperaments known as emotionality and introversion/extraversion.
- A knowledge of the origins of low self-esteem helps in understanding the student.
- Possible origins of low self-esteem are discussed.
- Both real and imaginary differences can be origins of low self-esteem.
- People vary in their tolerance of frustration. This is known as ego-strength.
- People use ego-defence mechanisms to protect themselves from experiencing hurt.
- Examples of common ego-defence mechanisms are discussed.

Further reading

Eysenck, H. J. (1977) *Psychology is about People*. Harmondsworth: Penguin.
Jung, C. G. (1921) *Psychological Types*. London: Routledge & Kegan Paul.

Chapter 3

The student with special educational needs

In the previous chapter tutors were introduced to the importance of getting to know something about the student's personal characteristics. These personal characteristics are combined into what is usually known as 'personality'. Equally important is the need to be aware of any special educational needs that a student may have. Without this knowledge the tutor may present the student with material that is difficult for them to learn or even totally beyond their capacity. If either of these were to happen, both tutor and student would become frustrated and the self-esteem of both would be at risk. Imagine for a moment the consequences of presenting a list of words to a student to learn without knowing that the student had a marked weakness in working memory! This weakness in working memory is often a symptom of dyslexia. Another example of the consequences of not knowing a student's special needs occurred during the monitoring of a county's remedial service. A tutor was beginning to show exasperation with a student who regularly appeared to be ignoring requests to complete homework. During the course of a later review the tutor discovered that the student had an undisclosed hearing loss. In this instance both tutor and student were subjected to stress that could have been avoided with a prior knowledge of the student's special educational needs.

An accurate assessment of each student's educational needs before beginning the tutoring prevents such difficulties occurring. A formal assessment is usually carried out before the tutoring is arranged, but not always. The tutor should always ascertain whether an assessment from a suitably qualified professional has been conducted to identify any special educational needs. Apart from the obvious value this would have when planning a learning programme, a student with special needs may require more intensive help with their self-esteem. They will already have experienced frustrations as a result of their limited literacy skills that will have negatively affected their self-esteem. The chances are that their low self-esteem will have been reduced even further as a consequence of the added frustrations arising from their specific learning difficulty.

The following are common types of special educational needs that tutors may encounter.

Hearing difficulties

The effect of a hearing loss on the social and emotional development of a person has been well documented in the literature. As oral communication plays a significant role in our kind of society, people who are deprived of this facility inevitably experience intense frustrations. A common source of this frustration stems from the negative reactions of others. It is a sad fact of life that people tend to become impatient with those who continually ask for information or instructions to be repeated. Such a student has probably met this challenge from people many times over and the chances are that they will have developed their own method of coping with it. Often they have developed a defensive attitude that can take the form of aggressive behaviour. This can be threatening to the tutor if not aware of its origins and they may take the behaviour personally. Once the behaviour is understood, the tutor can take the appropriate action, perhaps by ensuring that the student has opportunity to give the tutor adequate feedback so ensuring that they have been understood. Equally, some students with a hearing impairment may appear uninvolved or even apathetic and this can so easily be misinterpreted for lack of motivation. Whatever the reaction, the self-esteem of the student will be vulnerable and the tutor should be prepared for that. The individual behaviour of a student with a hearing impairment depends not only on their experiences in life but also, to a large extent, on the type and intensity of the hearing loss. Hearing impairment can vary tremendously across a continuum from being mildly hard of hearing in certain situations to being profoundly deaf in all situations. However, whatever the degree of disability, the student with a hearing impairment is generally more at risk of developing low self-esteem than the normally hearing student.

Visual difficulties

The effects of a visual impairment on the learning of literacy skills are well known and, as with a hearing loss, such an impairment can also vary along a continuum, from a partial loss of vision to complete blindness. Fortunately, a student with this disability is likely to have been diagnosed prior to coming for help with literacy skills. There is another type of visual problem, however, that often escapes diagnosis, perhaps because it is not so well known. Research has indicated that some people have trouble 'seeing print' despite there being no defect in visual acuity. These people often have not had a professional diagnosis of their difficulties, mainly as the research in this field is still relatively new. The evidence is building up that for these people the act of prolonged attention to print results in words appearing to move and the print becoming blurred. Not surprisingly this eventually brings on an intense headache. This syndrome has become known as 'scotopic sensitivity', which refers to a sensitivity to particular light frequencies, i.e. to different colours and different backgrounds. The most common form of this is a sensitivity to black on white, which of course is the media for most written material. People usually express relief when the condition has been diagnosed and then remedied by the use of either coloured lenses or by placing a coloured overlay on a page. Without a proper diagnosis of the problem, the frustrations experienced by the student can be so intense that they are put off reading altogether and self-esteem can be further reduced.

General learning difficulties

The interest in this kind of difficulty has been tremendous over many decades and has been the focus of much research and legislation. It has seen the rise in the intelligence test movement and the categorising and labelling of people according to their performance in these tests. This movement has had its critics and today considerable doubt is cast on the value of intelligence testing in education. Whatever the criticism, common observation tells us that some people appear to be 'quicker on the uptake' and quicker to solve problems than others and we usually think of this ability as 'intelligence'. It seems that students on literacy courses tend for the most part to have specific learning difficulties. However, there are also those students who have what has become known as a 'general learning difficulty'; they appear to be slower than most to learn in all areas. People can be placed along a continuum of ability in this respect with most appearing in the middle (see Figure 4, IQ distribution). When it comes to learning to read and to spell the research indicates that those known as having a learning difficulty can still learn to read and to spell properly. Their intellectual limitations do not have to prevent them from learning. However, it is also clear from the research that this group usually are slower than average to learn literacy skills, which is why they used to be known as 'slow learners'. When a general learning difficulty is suspected, it is important that tutors obtain a reliable estimate of a student's level of intelligence to prevent distress to the student by placing too many demands on them. Students with general learning difficulties need to be allowed to learn at their own pace. As with any student, if expected to work at a level beyond their present capabilities students with a general learning difficulty will become frustrated and self-esteem will be at risk.

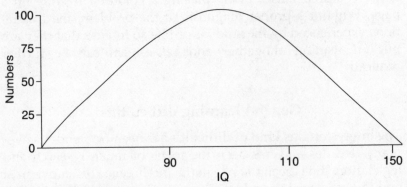

Figure 4   IQ distribution

The dyslexic student

There is another group of students that tutors in adult literacy classes are likely to come across from time to time. These are those students who demonstrate specific difficulties in working memory such that they find reading and spelling a difficult process. This condition is usually referred to as 'dyslexia'. Amongst any group of people with a reading or a spelling problem the chances are that there will be some with this specific learning difficulty. Estimates of the incidence of dyslexia suggest that 4 per cent of the population come into this category.

First let us define dyslexic. It is a much-abused term and has given rise to much argument and debate over the last couple of decades. The term commonly refers to a group of people with literacy difficulties who also show weaknesses in various aspects of information processing or working memory which result in their below average performance. This can apply to reading, writing or spelling. As it can take so many different forms as well as various degrees, it is not surprising that many professionals have refused to use the term, asserting that the definition of dyslexia has become so wide as to be meaningless. Unfortunately, most of the research and writings in this difficult area relate to children with very little of reference to the adult dyslexic. Currently, the Division of Educational and Child Psychologists of the British Psychological Society has decided to recommend the following definition:

> Dyslexia is evident when fluent and accurate word reading and/or spelling is learned very incompletely or with great difficulty.

This definition may be useful for children as it avoids reference to the origins of the condition, but it is hardly useful for the adult. Moreover, many bright adults have been able to learn basic literacy skills but their problem is usually slowness in using their skills. So often this is seen to be a function of weaknesses in auditory and/or visual memory. It is no wonder that many practitioners prefer the term 'specific learning difficulty' to describe this problem and so avoid completely the arguments regarding its origins.

Whatever the arguments for practitioners not using the term dyslexia, the inescapable fact is that dyslexia has been given recognition by the Department for Education and Employment as an official category of disability. Government grants are available in certain circumstances for those people diagnosed as dyslexic to enable them to purchase special equipment. They can also be granted special concessions in public examinations where their dyslexia puts them at an unfair disadvantage compared with their peers.

The reason why the dyslexic student often presents a special case in self-esteem tutoring resides in the use of the term itself. Reactions to having been diagnosed as dyslexic are not always predictable. To be told that you have something called 'dyslexia' can be quite alarming for many people whilst others can be relieved at the diagnosis. In my experience most dyslexics are bewildered when first given the news but the majority of these are relieved once it has been properly explained to them. The following extract from a conversation between a tutor and a dyslexic student illustrates some of the problems.

Tutor   . . . so this means that you have dyslexia.

Student   Oh dear! Is there any treatment I can have to get over it?

Tutor   I'm afraid not, although there are strategies you can learn to help you cope.

Student   I suppose it means I have some kind of brain damage. How could it happen?

Tutor   No, it does not necessarily mean that you are brain damaged, although some dyslexics indeed are brain damaged. The best way to look at it is to see it as something you have been born with which causes you to have a reading problem. It is usually inherited.

Student   Does this mean I got it from my parents?

Tutor   Well it could be from grandparents. The point is that it is in the genes.

Student   Oh! Well, I expect there are worse things to suffer from.

Tutor   Of course! Cheer up! We'll find you a tutor who specialises in this.

This student was left believing that he could be brain damaged with all the fears that might bring. A person with a vivid imagination could leave this conversation believing that they had some kind of condition of which they should be ashamed. In addition, they would be left wondering which of their ancestors were to blame for it! The psychologist was correct in saying that some dyslexics can be brain damaged but omitted to emphasise that the far greater majority of dyslexics would have no clinical evidence of this. In the face of this kind of interpretation it can be appreciated why the dyslexic may need careful counselling from the tutor. The second conversation between a tutor and a student is handled better but again illustrates the vulnerability of students diagnosed as dyslexic. This example also highlights the problem over how best to communicate to the student exactly what is meant by dyslexia.

Tutor	. . . so that means you are dyslexic.
Student	Oh dear! Is there anything I can do about it?
Tutor	Yes! Lots of things. But first, do you know what dyslexia means?
Student	I've heard of it but I'm not sure I understand exactly what it means.
Tutor	Well the main thing to understand is that it is not a medical condition and you don't need treatment. It is simply a word we use to describe students who have specific problems in learning to read and which have nothing to do with intelligence.
Student	I see. So why call it dyslexia? It does sound as if I have some kind of disease.
Tutor	Well, the reason we use the word is that research has shown that there are a number of people with reading and often spelling and writing problems who fail to make progress because of difficulties in certain areas of perception and information processing.
Student	What on earth does that mean? Information processing? Areas of perception?
Tutor	It means that some people are slower than others at interpreting what they see and what they hear and this is often because their immediate memory is poor.
Student	What do you mean by 'immediate memory'?
Tutor	Well, we all have a capacity to attend to information through our senses but some people are slower than

others in interpreting that information. This is because they cannot hold in their memory as many bits of information as other people.

Student   I suppose you are really saying I'm just slower than others. My teachers at school always said I was thick!

Tutor   NO! It has nothing to do with your intelligence. You are not thick.

Student   Oh! I give in.

Both the above conversations have been taken almost word for word from real-life case studies, and illustrate the need to help students come to terms with any diagnosis of their difficulties. Most tutors are well aware of this need to reassure their clients but some students need several sessions before they are fully comfortable with a diagnosis of dyslexia. This is especially the case where students have particularly low self-esteem. They will all have feelings of inadequacy as a result of their problems but some students have been known to be devastated when told that they are dyslexic. This is why the topic should always be dealt with by tutors early in the programme. It is important that students understand that dyslexia is not a medical condition and is simply a word used to describe difficulties associated with the learning of linguistic skills. Examples should be quoted of eminent people both in history and in contemporary life who have been diagnosed as dyslexic yet have become successful in their chosen fields.

The assistance of the psychologist who made the diagnosis may also be elicited in suitable cases. This would be especially appropriate where the students may ask for some elucidation of particular test results.

Summary

- Tutors should be acquainted with any special educational needs in students.
- Special educational needs can be either specific or general.
- Dyslexia is a specific learning difficulty of genetic origin.
- It is often demonstrated by a weakness in information processing.
- Dyslexia usually implies a difficulty with working memory.

- Tutors should explain to students that dyslexia is not a medical condition.
- Dyslexia is unrelated to intelligence.

Further reading.

Gilroy, D. E. and Miles T. R. (1996) *Dyslexia at College* (2nd edn). London: Routledge.
McLouglin, D. *et al.* (1994) *Adult Dyslexia*. London: Whurr.
Thomson, M. and Watkins, B. (1990) *Dyslexia: A Teaching Handbook*. London: Whurr.
Williams, E. G. (1965). *Vocational Counselling*. New York: McGraw-Hill.

Chapter 4

Assessing progress and maintaining motivation

People enrolled on basic literacy courses are usually those who have failed to acquire their literacy skills when at school. Returning to a formal learning environment and finding themselves once again in a teacher–pupil relationship can evoke past memories of schooldays. It is not surprising, therefore, that many of them show an initial apprehension as past memories of previous failures return. They are likely to worry that the inadequacies they regularly displayed as children in the classroom will be displayed once more. This places a heavy responsibility on the tutor to ensure that these feelings disappear early in the programme. As students develop rapport with their tutor and begin to appreciate the tutor's concern and the non-threatening atmosphere of an adult class, negative memories normally diminish. However, despite the establishment of a good rapport between student and teacher, the feelings may return from time to time, as early conditioning is a powerful process.

The introduction of any kind of assessment procedure is particularly likely to reawaken memories of past failure. This is even more likely where the student may have to undergo a formal examination. The thought of possible failure in these circumstances can result in downright panic in some instances and once again self-esteem is put at risk. Clearly, tutors should give this topic of assessment some serious thought. Some kind of assessment is usually required in order to plan programmes but this need not take the form of a formal examination. Continuous assessment throughout the course would be more preferable for this type of student rather than the more formal method of examination.

There are those students, of course, who have enrolled specifically with the intention of eventually entering a formal examination. These people may experience even more stress at the thought of an examination and so the relieving of their anxieties may require a more systematic approach than simply the establishment of rapport with the tutor. For this particular group of students the section on coping with stress outlined in Session 5 on page 83 should be introduced.

Maintaining motivation

The need to maintain students' motivation is a familiar task for tutors in colleges of further education. And students vary tremendously in their motivation for further study, depending mainly on whether they are there on a voluntary basis or whether they have been forced to attend. Some students will be on day-release schemes, often as a condition of their employment. These students can present a particular challenge as they may resent what they perceive as having to 'go back to school'. Motivation is never very high for these people, particularly in the beginning, as past feelings of failure are never far from their thoughts. The suggestion of examinations serves only to reduce their motivation even further as their anxiety levels are raised.

Many adults, however, have enrolled voluntarily and begin the course with enthusiasm and zest. But even these students can become quickly stressed at the thought of being examined or assessed. This may be one reason why students who have enrolled on a voluntary basis have such high drop-out rates. Their initial enthusiasm can quickly be lost if ways are not found to maintain motivation.

Tutors should be aware of the need for strategies for maintaining motivation on all basic literacy courses. This is readily recognised in primary and secondary schools but so often in further and adult education it is wrongly assumed that as these students are no longer children they will have an intrinsic motivation to learn. However, their emotional vulnerability, experiences of past failures and generally low self-esteem often mean that they are lacking in an inbuilt desire to learn.

It is useful to distinguish between the two sorts of motivation. First, **intrinsic motivation**, where the motivation comes from within the person. Those who are intrinsically motivated have been able to preserve their natural curiosity for learning new things. So with these people the task itself is of sufficient interest to stimulate them to learn. The second kind of motivation, **extrinsic motivation**, depends on external sources to maintain interest. Examples of external motivation with children might be material rewards for their efforts by receiving stars on their work, or even a bar of chocolate. With adults it is more likely to be monetary. The main point about external motivation is that the material rewards have to be earned, so they are given after the effort. It can be appreciated that, ideally, people should be motivated intrinsically and success in the task would be sufficient reward in itself. However, many adults on basic literacy courses are there to please relatives or friends, or are coerced to attend as mentioned earlier, and so intrinsic motivation is often lacking. Also, most are probably not wholly convinced that they will be able to learn, having had previous years of failure. In these instances, tutors may need to resort to a system of extrinsic motivation in the early days of the course. Most tutors will have devised their own strategies and will have their own techniques for maintaining motivation. Whatever these may be, the following principles should be considered as a theoretical basis for motivation.

1. Knowledge of results

There have been several experiments recorded over the years into providing students with immediate feedback on their progress as a means of maintaining motivation. The results of this research show that where students are made aware of their progress, their interest is maintained much longer. This may seem to be an obvious conclusion but in a busy session, with tutors sometimes having to take large groups, time often runs out before being able to do this. For maximum motivation the feedback should occur as soon as possible after the learning has taken place. The question that arises here is where progress may not have been made, whether the feedback of poor results would have an adverse effect. However, if the work has been broken down into sufficiently small steps then the student would normally be expected to achieve. Otherwise, of course, the feedback of results would have to be given with sensitivity. This highlights the importance of considering methods of motivation at the same time as the planning the learning programme.

2. Setting learning objectives

Students with low self-esteem usually have difficulty in setting goals for themselves in life generally. So it can be very therapeutic for them, as well as making their learning more efficient, if they can be shown how to set their own individual learning objectives. Objectives should be perfectly obtainable and based on the student's present levels of attainment. They should be sufficiently difficult to be challenging but not so hard that they are daunting. The student has to believe that the objectives are attainable. If the objectives are perceived by the student as unrealistic, the chances are that they will fail to achieve them and, of course, this would only serve to lower their self-esteem further. This is another reason why a prior assessment of a student's strengths and weaknesses is so important, as discussed in Chapter 3.

3. Keeping records

Most students will remember their schooldays when the teacher kept records of their progress and their test results. In the interests of enhancing self-esteem, however, it is suggested that where possible the keeping of records should be the responsibility of the student. This should be arranged even where the student may have a general learning difficulty and there may be some doubt about the student's ability to keep their own records. In those instances, both tutor and student could keep records. Generally this should take the form of a graph of their progress over the term as illustrated in Figure 5.

The plateau between weeks 3 and 4 is usual. This is when the material learned is being consolidated and this phenomenon should be explained to the student.

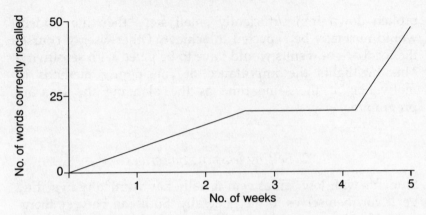

Figure 5 Graph of student's progress

4. Personality factors

In Chapter 2 emphasis was placed on the need for tutors to understand differences in students' temperaments. When it comes to maintaining motivation, the research shows that there are considerable differences between the way people are motivated to learn as well as in their responses to the same learning experience. These differences appear to be detemined by their different temperaments. For instance, it seems that extraverts become bored much more quickly than introverts. Moreover, introverts work best alone or in a one-to-one situation. Extraverts are happier working in groups with other people around them. Unless tutors are aware of these findings they may inadvertently place a student in a situation in which they are temperamentally unsuited to learn. An introvert having to work in a noisy environment with other people will underachieve, with the risk of a further lowering of self-esteem. The extravert, on the other hand, is not going to be motivated to achieve if having to work in isolation for a lengthy period, with an equal lowering of self-esteem.

5. Homework

Most tutors will expect their students to do homework between the sessions. This is where tutors will have to be patient, particularly with students with very low self-esteem. Once again, it is their past experiences that will largely determine students' attitudes. Many will have learned that homework equals pain, and old habits die hard. Tutors must be prepared, therefore, for some students to procrastinate for a while. Provided tutors are prepared for this and for students to come with excuses for not having done homework during the early part of the course they are not likely to react so negatively. Of course, if the student continues to avoid doing homework, eventually they will have to be confronted with the problem.

Some students might welcome a few hints on study skills to help them maintain their motivation when having to do homework. The following could be among these hints:

1. Stick to a regular time each day for the homework.
2. Have regular break periods for refreshment.
3. Reward yourself after each homework session, e.g. a trip to see a friend etc.

Formal examinations

Eventually, some students will be faced with the task of a formal examination. This can be an unnerving experience for many people, and for a person already lacking in confidence it can be particularily daunting. Anxieties engendered in these people by the mere thought of a forthcoming examination can range from mild apprehension to a full-blown panic attack. It is important that tutors are aware of the anxious student as there is research evidence to show that anxiety interferes with thinking, so it is almost inevitable that the anxious student will underperform in an examination.

Anxiety can be controlled if this type of student is supported and well prepared in advance for the examination. Students should be made aware in good time of the logistics of the examination, such as the time, the setting and the procedure. However, it is also encumbent on the tutor to allay the students' anxieties. This should not be too difficult a task as by the time the examination becomes a reality, tutors will have generally come to know their students fairly well. Consequently, students are probably only too glad to be able to discuss any anxiety feelings. If the anxiety is severe the methods of coping with stress outlined in Session 5 on page 83 should prove helpful.

Summary

- Low self-esteem students are likely to feel threatened by formal assessments.
- Strategies for the maintenance of motivation should be considered.
- Homework is a particular source of distress for many students.
- Personality factors influence students' motivation.
- Student anxiety over examinations needs special attention.

Further reading

Case, F. (1993) *How To Study: A Practical Guide.* Basingstoke: Macmillan.

Gilroy, D. E. (1995) Stress factors in the college student. In Miles, T. R. and Varma, V. P. (eds.) *Dyslexia and Stress.* London: Whurr.

Leader, D. (1990) *How To Pass Exams.* Cheltenham: Thorne.

Peelo, M. (1994) *Helping Students with Study Problems.* Buckingham: Open University.

Chapter 5

Developing the skills

In this chapter tutors are shown how to develop the specific communication skills considered by the research to be essential for enhancing self-esteem in students – **acceptance, genuineness** and **empathy**. The development of these skills in tutors will not only help their students towards higher self-esteem but should also assist in the raising of their own.

During the initial stages, the tutor–student relationship is generally a formal one. As the course continues the relationship tends to becomes less formal and, with the development of their communication skills, tutors should begin to feel freer to relate to their students on a more personal level. The significance of the personal relationship is emphasised here as it is the quality of this relationship that is the key to successful self-esteem enhancement. Without meaning to devalue the tutor's technical teaching role, it is the teacher as *a person* who is going to be the most effective. The self-esteem enhancement approach requires tutors to develop in themselves the qualities of acceptance, genuineness and empathy within a supportive framework. Not only does the development of these qualities enhance the communication skills of the tutor, it also ensures that the tutor presents to the students a high self-esteem model.

The modelling effect

People will tend to model themselves on those whom they like and with whom they have a close relationship. The research shows that a high self-esteem person can positively affect a low self-esteem person once they have made a warm trusting relationship with them. Moreover, this seems to happen unconsciously, without their being aware of it. I am reminded of the story of Douglas Bader, the former Second World War fighter pilot who was renowned for his high self-esteem and enthusiasm. When a prisoner of war in the infamous Colditz prison camp, he regularly called meetings with his fellow prisoners. The other prisoners are reported as saying that they always left these meetings feeling that they 'had had cocktails'. The confident, high self-esteem of Bader was infectious. Tutors of high self-esteem, who have established warm relationships with their students can also do this. This places a responsibility on tutors to ensure they do have high self-esteem themselves. This means not only possessing those essential qualities of acceptance, genuineness and empathy, but also being enthusiastic, confident, and happy people in their own lives.

Acceptance, genuineness and empathy

The following exercises and activities are designed to help tutors develop this high self-esteem model. Ideally, they should be practised in the company of a fellow tutor.

Acceptance

The quality of acceptance means being able to accept the person unconditionally even if you disagree with their views, or even with their behaviour. It means being able to communicate that you accept them for who they are, and recognise their right to be respected as a unique individual. This quality is probably the most difficult of the three to develop in those who do not have it to start with. The reason for this is that an accepting attitude implies the possession of an attitude of mind and a philosophy of life rather than a particular skill. It is more a question of values than skills, values that have been developed throughout life. It implies a liking for people and a sincere concern for their welfare without being sentimental about it. For instance, it may not always be easy to accept a student if they express views which are radically different from the tutor's. This does not mean that the tutor should change their views but it does mean that they have to accept the right of the student to have different views. Tutors who are accepting will be able to separate the views they do not like from the person. The person is entitled to respect even if their views are different. An interesting point about being accepting is that we cannot easily pretend to be accepting if we are not genuinely so – our body language will give us away. Tone of voice, body posture, facial expressions, hand gestures, all express our real feelings and it is body language to which people mainly react. Experiments have shown that body language is remembered long after the verbal message has been forgotten. Moreover, it is the body language that people react to on first meeting, and first impressions tend to stick! So you cannot fool people if you are not genuinely accepting of them.

Exercise in accepting different views
This exercise consists of statements designed to elicit discussion and alert tutors to the fact that people sometimes do have different views but that they should be accepted. Two tutors discuss the following:

- Some people are innately bad.
- There is no such thing as a 'criminal personality'.
- Society does not have the main role to play in people turning to crime.
- Students have a right to express negative views.
- Some people are just difficult and time can be wasted trying to get on with them.
- The emphasis in prisons should be on punishment not on reformation.

Genuineness

To be genuine is to be unafraid to be yourself. It means being able to express opinions which may not be popular. It means being able to behave in the way you feel you want to behave no matter if others disapprove. Generally, people in our kind of society tend to be wary of expressing their true selves in a relationship until they feel they are trusted. There is probably a cultural factor here also as, for instance, the English are renowned for being more reserved than their Latin neighbours. So they will say the 'conventional' thing and perhaps introduce themselves by discussing a 'safe' subject such as the weather. Obviously there are degrees of this with some people being reserved to such an extent that they rarely, if ever, express their true selves. Carl Jung referred to this as wearing a persona (mask). You never really get to know some people who wear a strong persona. Whilst this places these people at risk mentally, as they become cut off from their 'real selves', it also gets in the way of communication. This is is why genuineness is considered to be such an essential aspect of counselling. If tutors are poor communicators they will be at a disadvantage when talking to students. There is reason to try to develop genuineness. This is because people who are not genuine are not so easily trusted by others. As they generally project a conventional image it is not easy to know who they really are so neither do you really know where you stand with them. You never know whether they agree with you as so often they 'sit on the fence'. So you don't trust them and as a consequence you in turn are reluctant to reveal your true self. Without genuineness there is no real communication and as self-esteem enhancement involves a modelling process, i.e. students will model themselves on the tutors, it is self-evident that the tutor who is not genuine is not easily going to enhance self-esteem.

Empathy

This is is considered by many to be the essence of counselling. In the context of self-esteem enhancement it means tutors being able to put themselves in the place of the student and so being able to feel what they feel. It is obvious that nobody can completely feel another person's experience unless they have been in the same circumstances but it should be possible to share their feelings to some degree and to be able to communicate this. Tutors who can empathise are able to build a bridge between themselves and the student. This is experienced by the student as a feeling of support and of being understood. It depends largely on the tutor being a good listener but in addition it means being able to communicate to the student that the tutor feels what the student is going through. Some people do this naturally but with practice it can be developed in those who do not at first find it easy.

For some people empathy is a quality that seems to develop naturally as they go through life. These people have learned to become sensitive to the distress and suffering around them. They quickly seem able to understand the problems of others and to be able to appreciate them from the point of view of the other person. A word of caution should be inserted at this point; empathy does not mean identification. If they were to identify it would mean they would become like the other person. Empathy means having a deep understanding of the other person but without losing your own identity. Carl Rogers has said that 'this is the most precious gift that one can give to another'. To be able to do this implies that the counsellor is strong in their identity and so has high self-esteem.

Through the process of empathy the client feels trusted and valued and so sufficiently secure to be able to express problems. But of course empathy means more than that; it can set off what Carl Jung called a healing process which allows feelings to be expressed which have previously been blocked. Where the tutor is empathic, students will find that they are able to talk about their fears and anxieties over their literacy difficulties, perhaps for the first time, and in so doing find that they are not as bad as they thought. People can think about how to resolve their problems but it is only when they can express them with emotion that they can begin to come to terms with them, and this is what happens in an empathic relationship. This is why empathy is probably the most essential ingredient in any kind of counselling relationship. It certainly helps if the tutor can empathise with the student.

As both the quality of empathy and the quality of genuineness are considered crucial in enhancing self-esteem, the following exercises are presented to illustrate the qualities through conversations between a tutor and a student.

Exercise in being genuine
One tutor plays the role of the student while the other plays the tutor. Roles should be reversed for the second part of the exercise so that both have the experience of acting the student.

Scene 1 – without genuineness

Tutor   Good morning! I am Mr Jones and have been appointed
         to be your tutor.

Student Good morning! I am pleased to meet you.

Tutor   You will be attending here once a week on a Wednes-
         day at 7 p.m. Is that OK for you?

Student Yes, that will be fine by me.

Tutor   Course books will be provided but you should bring
         your own writing paper and pen.

Student I see.

Tutor   Right! We might as well get started. Before we begin I
         need to know the kind of errors you make in
         your spelling so I would like to give you a short test.
         OK?

Student Yes, go ahead.

Tutor   (After testing). Now let's see how you got on.

Student I know I've done badly. I have always had a problem
         with spelling.

Tutor   Lots of students have that problem.

Student I hate having to do tests.

Tutor   Well we do need to know your level of attainment.

Student I understand, but it is not easy for me.

Tutor   These results show me where to start in the tutoring.

Student I see.

Tutor   Right. Now let's talk about some homework. You need
         to do some exercises at home.

This conversation was very professional with the tutor explaining clearly what was required. However, the relationship lacked
something. Contrast it with the next conversation.

Scene 2 – with genuineness

Tutor   Good morning! My name is David Jones and I am here
         to help you with your spelling.

Student Good morning, I'm John Davis, I'm pleased to meet
         you.

Tutor   It must be a bit hard for you having to do some study
         after working all day.

Student Yes, it is a bit. I suppose I am a bit tired but I'll cope.

Tutor   It's all right for me – I usually manage to get an afternoon nap when I work in the evenings.

Student   I can't do that in my job.

Tutor   No, I understand that. I admire students who manage to come here after a day's work. Right! If you are ready I would like to give you a few spellings just to see the kind of problems you have. That will help me to know how best to help you.

Student   That's fine by me. Ready when you are.

Tutor   (having given the test) Not bad. I can see you have made a few mistakes but now I know where to begin to help you.

Student   I'm not very good, am I? I feel so silly. Do you think I can catch up?

Tutor   I'm sure you can. Everybody feels a bit nervous coming back to study after being away from it for a few years. I remember when I tried to learn French, I was hopeless at first.

Student   OK, I think I'll give it a go.

Tutor   Great! By the way, will you have time to do some homework?

Student   Yes, if you think I need it.

Tutor   Well, it does help. I remember how it helped me when I was doing those French lessons.

In this scene the tutor brought his own personal experiences into the conversation. This had the effect of the student opening up and a human relationship developing as distinct from the purely professional, tutor–student one of the previous scene. The student is more likely to trust the tutor and so the modelling process is more likely to occur. In Scene 2 the tutor related to the student as a human being first and only after that as a tutor. As a result, the student feels encouraged and not threatened. The kind of relationship established in Scene 1 would have reminded the student of schooldays and so of past failures. The tutor in Scene 1 came across as an expert – as a teacher – and not as a human being with possible failings. This kind of relationship would only reinforce low self-esteem. In Scene 2 self-esteem is not threatened and a new positive attitude to the self is begun.

Exercise 1 in empathy
This skill is usually considered to be the most essential skill possessed by the professional counsellor. People differ in their capacity to empathise but it is a skill that can be learned with practice.

Scene 1 – without empathy

Tutor   Your homework was done well but I noticed a few errors in the spelling

Student   Oh dear! Is that serious? (feeling worried)

Tutor   Not really. It's nothing that you can't put right. See here
          . . .

Student   I see. (brightening up but still concerned)

Tutor   Now I want you to try this one, OK?

Student   All right, I just hope I can do this one properly. (worried over possible repeat failure)

Tutor   Just try it. Do your best

Student   Right, here goes, but don't be surprised if I get it wrong again. (getting anxious)

Tutor   Let's have a look.

Student   I know I've made a mess of it again, haven't I? (feeling silly)

Tutor   Well, it's not quite right. Let's see if we can do it again, shall we?

Scene 2 – with empathy

Tutor   Your homework was done well but I noticed a few errors in the spelling.

Student   Oh dear, is that serious?

Tutor   You sound worried. It's OK, you'll soon be able to put it right.

Student   I was a bit worried I'd make a mess of the whole thing.

Tutor   You must have been a bit nervous at first but that's normal. It's OK to make mistakes.

Student   I don't want to keep making these silly errors.

Tutor   It's natural to be anxious like that at first, but you will become more confident with time.

Student   I feel so angry when I make that kind of mistake. I am so stupid.

Tutor You are bound to feel angry with yourself but you are trying so hard so perhaps you should pat yourself on the back for that.

Student You are right. I am trying hard.

Tutor That's more like it! Now you sound determined to master it, and I'm sure you will.

In Scene 1 the tutor failed to listen to the student's feelings and dealt with the student's comments logically. This did nothing either to enhance self-esteem or to reduce the student's anxiety. In Scene 2 the tutor was careful to listen to how the student was feeling so the student felt understood and supported. Anxiety was reduced as a result, and self-esteem was maintained. Provided that the tutor possesses the qualities of acceptance, genuineness and empathy, the tutor will find it easy to establish a natural relationship within which the student will feel secure and valued.

The tutor who is able to be empathic will use what is known as active listening. This means listening to the feelings behind the words in a conversation and being able to reflect these back to the student. For example, if the student were to say, 'I don't find this book very interesting', ask yourself what the student is feeling when saying this. Is the student feeling angry, or upset? Is the student feeling inadequate? Is the student simply bored? Whatever the feelings behind the words it is important that the tutor reacts to them. The student's body language will usually give a clue to this. If the perceived feeling is one of inadequacy then the tutor might reply 'I can see that you are finding this hard, but all students do at first. I know you will eventually manage it.' The student will have been reassured and also will feel supported by realising that the tutor understands their real feelings about the book. In active listening the tutor does two things, firstly conveys to the student an accurate understanding of their feelings, and secondly gives some words of encouragement.

Exercise 2 in empathy (for two tutors)
This is best done in two parts as follows:
1. A tells B of an event in their life which caused them some emotion at the time. This does not need to be anything too dramatic!

B interrupts at the end of two or three sentences and tries to paraphrase A's words.

A confirms, or corrects, B's attempt to paraphrase and continues with the story.

B again interrupts after two or three sentences and again attempts to paraphrase.

A again confirms or corrects B's attempt to paraphrase.

After about five minutes A and B should reverse their roles.

2. A continues with the story or begins another one if so desired.

B tries to listen for the emotions A must have felt during the emotional event.

B interrupts after two minutes and reflects back to B these guessed feelings.

A confirms or corrects the accuracy of this reflection.

It is important that this skill is put into practice as soon as possible after this exercise, reflecting feelings back to the student where appropriate, e.g. 'You must have been feeling pretty embarrassed when that happened'.

Communication checklist

After having given due consideration to the qualities of acceptance, genuineness and empathy, tutors might like to assess these skills in themselves using the following checklist and so decide how much work is needed in developing these qualities. Tutors should ask themselves if they:

- use eye contact (but not a fixed stare!)?
- remember to smile when appropriate?
- use a harsh or aggressive voice?
- always sit in a relaxed manner?
- are able to reflect the student's feelings when necessary?
- are able to paraphrase some of the students' words as an aid to empathy?
- encourage the student to express opinions and feelings?
- seek oppportunities to show they trust the student?
- are able to express their own feelings and opinons.?
- are able to reveal their own background and interests.?
- communicate to the students that they are interested in them?

Becoming sensitive to non-verbal cues

As we become older we tend to be less sensitive to non-verbal behaviour, or body language as it is often called. Children and animals are very sensitive to how others look and how others sound. Without a word being spoken children know whether the adults around them like them or not. With practice we can regain this lost skill as adults. It is especially useful for tutors to be able to pick up messages from the student's body language as low self-esteem people do not find it easy to express themselves verbally. Successful communication between people depends as much on the non-verbal message as on the verbal one. The research shows that following a lecture people remember what the lecturer looked and sounded like long after they have forgotten what was actually said!

Exercise in observing body language
In as natural a manner as possible while tutoring, the tutor should observe the student's body language, noting the following:

- speed of movement, i.e. rushes in or walks slowly;
- facial expressions, i.e. smiles easily or in a forced manner, mouth is tight or relaxed;
- general body movements, i.e. sits calmly or wriggles;
- hand movements, i.e. stiff or relaxed;
- general posture.

Notes should be made on the above observations from memory immediately *after* the session.

Exercise in reading emotions
Two tutors should each take turns in acting out the following emotions without speaking while the other guesses it:

amused	repulsed
attracted	hostile
contented	depressed
excited	fearful
overjoyed	angry
proud	guilty
happy	anxious
loving	disappointed

A self-help approach to developing confidence as a tutor

Working in the field of human relationships is a potentially stressful occupation and teaching adults literacy skills is a perfect example of this. Adjusting emotionally to different personalities can become exhausting and if tutors become overtired they are at risk of losing confidence in themselves. It is important therefore that tutors in this area of work recognise that they are in a high risk profession and learn how to protect themselves from stress.

The work of Albert Ellis is particularly relevant in this context. He has developed a system of counselling which he calls **Rational-Emotive Therapy** which readily lends itself to being used as a method of self-improvement. The basis of this system is that we are all responsible for our own emotions and our thinking causes our emotions. If someone insults us, we may say 'He made me angry' when the fact of the matter is that we made ourselves angry by the way in which we interpreted the situation. As an illustration of this, supposing a drunk is staggering down a street and bumps into somebody. This might be interpreted by one person as a pure accident and the drunk seen as a harmless individual. Another person, in contrast, might regard the incident as deliberate and see the drunk as a sinister figure. People often interpret the same event in different ways according to how they think about the situation and in so doing they experience different emotions.

There may be times when a tutor starts to feel inadequate, perhaps because their student is not making much progress, and they may leave the sessions feeling a bit depressed. Ellis would say that they are making themselves depressed by how they are interpreting the situation. If they can make the effort to interpret things in a positive way their depression would be minimised and with practice should disappear altogether. The key to this is being able to change interpretations of events by what Ellis calls 'disputation'. This involves deliberately changing the negative beliefs for positive ones, which entails analysing the situation into thinking, feeling and behaviour. Ellis calls this system the ABCDE method and it is in two stages. The following example illustrates how the system might be employed in the hypothetical case of a tutor feeling depressed after being criticised by a student.

Stage 1: The tutor analyses the situation

A = *Activating event*	B = *Beliefs*	C = *Consequences*
Student complains that the tutor is not being sufficiently helpful so they are not making progress	'I am no good at this job. I am a total failure.'	'I feel so depressed.'

Stage 2: The treatment

D = *Disputation*	E = *Effect*
'Where is the evidence that I am no good at this job and that I am a total failure? Perhaps I am not going as well as I could at the moment but I have had other successes in life. I could improve my skills here. Anyway I cannot be a total failure just because of one criticism. That is not being rational.'	'I am sorry that the student feels that I am no good as a tutor but I cannot be responsible for his feelings. That would be irrational. I am going to improve my teaching skills so I can become a better tutor. I am sad that this incident occurred but I have no reason to be depressed.'

In Stage 2 it is essential to be able to take a scientific and logical attitude for the beliefs and then to change the beliefs accordingly, so that any irrational thinking is substituted by rational thinking. Also, it is important that the new rational thinking is rehearsed regularly for maximum effect.

There may be times when tutors have other kinds of problems that are causing them to lose confidence in themselves. If so, they should analyse the situation exactly as outlined under the headings of ABCDE in the illustration. It cannot be emphasised enough that this approach is dependent on being able to think clearly and rationally. This is more likely to be achieved if two tutors can combine their efforts. That way the one can ensure that the other is thinking logically about the problem. It is all too easy to become bogged down in irrational thinking and it is much easier to renounce this with help from a colleague.

Checklist of tutor skills

Tutors should complete the following checklist of skills some time after their first session:

- Did you feel that you gave the student respect?
- Did the conversation flow easily?

- Did you feel relaxed throughout the session?
- Were you able to reassure the student where necessary?
- Were you able to reveal to the student anything about yourself?
- Do you feel you know how this student feels about the session?
- Did you have an opportunity to praise the student?
- Did you feel that you were in control of the session?
- Do you feel you would like to see the student for another session?

The tutor should aim to be able to answer Yes to all these questions.

Summary

- Students tend to model their self-esteem on the tutors.
- The qualities of acceptance, genuineness and empathy are required.
- Tutors should assess their skills on the communications checklist.
- Awareness of non-verbal behaviour needs to be practised.
- Tutors can become more confident using the ABCDE approach (Ellis).

Further reading

Argyle, M. (1996) *Psychology of Interpersonal Behaviour*. Harmondsworth: Penguin.

Branden, M. *Six Pillars of Self-Esteem*. London: Bantam.

Ellis, A. (1993) *How to Stubbornly Refuse to Make Yourself Miserable about Anything*. Australia: McMillan.

Priestley, P. and McGuire, J. (1983) *Learning to Help*. London: Tavistock.

Chapter 6

The tutoring session

Whilst each tutor will organise their sessions in terms of their own personalities and every situation is likely to be different, there are some basic principles which are common to all sessions.

The setting

There is some research evidence to show that attitudes are more easily changed where the person attempting to effect attitude change has status in the eyes of the client. As one of the aims of the tutoring is to change students' attitudes towards themselves, the status of the tutor is going to be an important factor. It follows that the sessions should therefore take place in comfortable, private surroundings where there are not likely to be any interruptions. It would be difficult for the student to perceive the tutor as having much status if the sessions were to take place in uncomfortable, poorly furnished rooms.

The materials

Tutors will normally have their own ideas regarding reading materials and records. In addition to these it is useful to have a separate booklet to record any salient points from their conversations with the student. The reason for keeping these notes is to remind the tutor of what was discussed at each session. It is so easy to forget the content of the sessions unless notes are kept. It is advisable that these notes be made after the student has left and not in their company. They should be read again before the student arrives for the next session. Having read them the tutor will be in a receptive frame of mind should the student wish to refer to what was discussed in the previous session.

Meeting the student

Tutors would normally have interviewed the students before the first session. The main procedures of the course would have been explained at this initial meeting and tutor and student would have begun the process of getting to know each other. The materials and methods used will be explained at this first meeting, as well as the length of the sessions and their times. All this is straightforward and should not present any problems either to the student or to the tutor. The subject of self-esteem enhancement would not normally be raised at the first session. The need for tutors to use part, or all, of the Self-Esteem Enhancement Programme would only become evident in future sessions as the tutor gets to know the student.

Students with literacy difficulties usually feel apprehensive at the first sesson so an important aim of the first meeting should be to ensure that the student feels at ease and in no way feels threatened by the forthcoming programme. As the sessions progress, students will begin to talk more freely and indeed in time they will most likely confide in the tutor any problems they may have. It should be emphasised therefore at the first meeting that anything that may be said during the sessions will be regarded as confidential and would not go beyond the tutor. Of course, should a student confide something criminal, common sense should prevail and confidence may need to be broken.

The quiet student

Most students will eventually open up and chat freely with their tutor as their early anxieties over the sessions disappear. However, the stage at which a student feels sufficiently confident to do this will vary considerably. Some students may take a long time to open up and it is important in these cases that the tutor does not hurry the process and put undue pressure on the student by frequent questioning. An important reason for not questioning the student directly is that it infringes their right to have private thoughts and so places them in an inferior position, the reverse of self-esteem enhancing.

It is tempting to ask direct questions, especially where the tutor might have reason to suspect that the student has a certain area of stress. There is a misguided view prevalent that people with a problem always feel better if they 'get it off their chest' by talking about it. This view is an outdated relic of the old Freudian psychology that in order to come to terms with a problem it was necessary to reveal all, especially the past. It is now recognised by most modern counsellors that this is not necessary and in fact in some cases can be harmful. It can be helpful to people to express their areas of stress to a person who can empathise with them, but only when they are ready and want to bring up the subject.

It is not always easy to resist trying to draw a student out by questions. It is tempting under those circumstances to ask questions like 'What did you do this weekend?' or even 'Is there anything worrying you?' Whilst generally no harm would come from such direct questioning it is not going to enhance self-esteem. A far better plan where the student is not forthcoming is to stick to the principles of active listening by saying something like 'You seem to be a bit quiet today' or 'I find that students often feel a bit nervous at first, but you'll soon feel OK'.

Occasionally, a student who wishes to talk may then demonstrate more severe personal problems. As the object of self-esteem enhancement tutoring is not to attempt to unravel deep-rooted personality difficulties, in these circumstances the tutor should suggest seeking the help of a suitably-qualified professional.

It is interesting to observe children in the kind of situation where there is little conversation. Children are much more comfortable with silences. Adults always seem uneasy with silences and have to fill them with words. Remember, if you have an adult student who does not talk easily, much communication takes place non-verbally. The student will know by your body language whether you approve of them. Silences can be unnerving, particularly with a relative stranger. Where we know the person well it is not unusual to have silent periods between speech and generally this is not threatening. Whenever a tutor feels threatened by a student's silence it is natural to wonder if there is something wrong. In such cases it is helpful for the tutor to apply the following mental checklist:

- Is this student unwell?
- Is the student feeling shy?
- Is the student afraid?
- Is the student a naturally quiet person?

If the student does appear to be unwell then obviously the tutor should take appropriate action according to the symptoms presented. Where the answer is that the student seems to be afraid or shy then the tutor should offer reassurance. As a first step, admiration might be expressed that the student had the courage to enrol and do something about their literacy difficulties. Every effort should be made to put the student at ease without pressing them to talk.

Some students may be naturally quiet. In other words they may be the natural introverts as discussed in Chapter 2. In this case they will be relaxed, although quiet. If the tutor is extraverted in temperament, this behaviour will appear to be strange. Even so, it is still important to respect the student's different personality and not to become irritated or anxious by their quietness.

The low self-esteem student who seems to be shy either lacks social skills, is demonstrating extreme lack of confidence, or perhaps both.

Exercise in role-playing the quiet student
This is a useful activity for tutors as it gives them practice in facing the student who does not talk easily. Two tutors should take part: the first tutor takes the role of the quiet student and the second is the tutor interviewing the student for the first time and explaining the course. The interview should go on for no more than five minutes with the student hardly responding at all. The tutor has to decide on the reason for the student's reticence and react accordingly. The student should decide in advance the reason for their reticence. After five minutes the tutors discuss the role-playing and then repeat with the roles reversed.

The over-talkative student

Those students who talk too much can also present problems, although they are easier to deal with than the silent ones.

However, they can talk so much that they monopolise the session. These students could be reacting for the same reasons as the reticent students only whereas the reticent ones are likely to have introverted temperaments and so be reacting to frustration in an introverted fashion, these over-talkative people are likely to have extraverted temperaments and so be reacting to frustration in an extraverted fashion. Tutors should ask themselves the following questions if presented with the kind of student who talks too much:

- Is this student feeling anxious about the situation?
- Is this student compensating for feelings of inadequacy?'
- Is this student feeling aggressive?
- Is this student simply lacking in social skills?
- Is this student a naturally extraverted person?

As with the reticent student, the way in which the tutor deals with this behaviour depends on the answers to the above questions. Whatever the answers may be, the first step is to interrupt the student's flow of words. Ask the student, 'Do you mind if I ask you a few questions?' and without waiting for a reply ask several, such as 'Where do you live? Which school did you attend?', and so on. This is easier if a checklist of questions has already been prepared. The next step is to keep the student focused on the point of the session by repeating the object of the session. It may be necessary to do this several times at intervals.

Exercise in role-playing the over-talkative student
Again, two tutors should take part. The first tutor takes the role of the over-talkative student and tries to monopolise the session. The second tutor tries to guess the reason for the behaviour and reacts as suggested above. After five minutes the roles are reversed so each has a turn at being the over-talkative student.

Handling the session

Reinforcing the positive

Praise is a powerful means of enhancing self-esteem but it has to be used wisely and honestly. To praise a person dishonestly results either in scorn from the other person or a false self-image. Either way it does not enhance self-esteem. Enhancing self-esteem means more than just praising and being nice to people. It means first of all giving people a realistic image of themselves.

Tutors need to be alert for comments from the student which justify praise. This is called giving positive reinforcement. An obvious example would be where a student has just shown that they have learned something new or produced an excellent piece of work. Another instance where praise might be offered is in connection with something the student might tell the tutor about an outside activity which is praiseworthy. For example, the student might have been involved in some kind of public event, or even merely having successfully accomplished a domestic task. It would be natural to offer praise under such circumstances. However, tutors need to be prepared for the low self-esteem student who rejects the praise and denies that they are worthy of it. This is a not an uncommon reaction. Indeed, children of low self-esteem when praised are likely to destroy the work that is admired. The reason for this is that we all feel vaguely insecure when suddenly having to perceive ourselves in a different light from what we are used to. The same phenomenon applies with the low self-esteem adult, although they have usually learned not to react so violently. The tutor should not argue the point when this happens but merely reassert quietly that, even so, they consider the work worthy of praise, and then change the subject. This does not mean giving up praising the student in the future; quite the contrary. It means simply recognising that low self-esteem people need time to change their image of themselves. So the same procedure should be continued the next time the student is worthy of praise. Eventually, as the sessions develop, the student will begin to perceive themselves in a more positive light.

Although praising these activities can be positively reinforcing there is another, more powerful means of enhancing self-esteem. This is, in effect, praising the personality of the student. People feel particularly valued when they know that the person they identify with likes them and finds them interesting. It is important therefore that the tutor tries to find an appropriate occasion to convey this liking. Obviously, again, this should be done sensitively and naturally otherwise it will not only sound odd but could easily be misconstrued! Comments such as 'I look forward to these sessions . . . you are an interesting person to talk to' are preferable to 'I like you . . . I like your personality'.

Understanding not patronising

It is all too easy when confronted by somebody in distress to be patronising. It is natural for most of us to show sympathy but unless this is accompanied by some understanding of the problems it can be reduced to sentimental patronising. People in distress do not need to be told that they are deserving of sympathy. They do need to know in this case that the tutor understands them and this is where the power of empathy is felt. If the tutor merely sympathises with them over having a reading difficulty they may feel some comfort but they will not be changing their attitude to themselves. Remember that in self-esteem tutoring the aim is to help the students feel more positive about themselves, so if the tutor hears a student expressing self-pity, whilst they should listen actively they should not agree with the sentiments. This does not mean that the tutor should argue the point. It means listening and then making some comment to show that the tutor understands. In other words, empathising with the student's feelings and then making a positive comment, such as 'I can see that your reading difficulty is upsetting for you. Now let's see what we can do about it'. In order to achieve a change of self-concept it is necessary to give up old attitudes towards oneself, so every opportunity should be taken by the tutor to show understanding but not by dwelling on negative feelings. Sympathy does not have a role to play in self-esteem enhancement and should not be mistaken for empathy.

Empowering the student

There is a concept in psychology known as **locus of control**. This refers to the extent to which people feel they have control over their lives. Most people have learned that through their own efforts they can have some impact on what happens to them, although of course nobody can have total control over their lives. There are many chance events in life that we all encounter at some stage. Some people, however, do feel that they have total control over their lives and this group are said to be 'internally controlled'. When they succeed they are firmly convinced that they did so because of their own efforts. However, by the same token, if they fail an examination for instance, perhaps because of poor lecturing, they still believe they were responsible.

There is another group, said to be 'externally controlled', that believes that they have absolutely no control over their lives. If they succeed, they believe that they were just lucky. If they fail, then they automatically blame somebody or something else. Clearly, both these extreme views are unhealthy and most people are a bit of each, recognising that chance does play a part in life. The point about this for the purposes of self-esteem enhancement is that the research shows that people who have low self-esteem usually are also those who are mainly externally controlled. This is probably a result of continual failure. In tutoring, anything which helps students to see that they can have some control over their lives is likely to enhance self-esteem, and ultimately their literacy skills.

Encouraging students to keep their own progress records would be one way of developing this characteristic; other ways may occur to the tutor as they get to know their students. However, mention must be made of one powerful method of encouraging internal locus of control. This occurs naturally when students ask for advice. In the rather intense relationships which can be established in these tutoring sessions, students may confide in the tutor about a particular personal problem and ask for advice. Although the solution to the problem may be obvious to the tutor, the giving of advice should be resisted. No harm would come from giving advice but in so doing an opportunity will have been missed to help the student come to their own decision and so become more internally controlled. If a student asks for advice the tutor should try to phrase a reply in such a way that the student is forced to come to their own conclusion – phrases like, 'What do you think would be the best thing to do?' 'Have you thought of trying something else?' 'I once knew somebody who did . . .'.

If despite trying to help students come to a solution themselves they remain unable to do so, then the tutor might give their answer to the problem but still not actually say what the student should do. For instance, the tutor might say, 'I once had this problem and I did . . .'. The aim is to help the student become responsible for their own behaviour and to see that their efforts really do make a difference.

Expectancy effect

This is a powerful phenomenon in any tutor–student relationship. It refers to the attitude of expectancy possessed by the tutor regarding a student's potential to make progress. In essence, tutors who expect their students to make progress are likely to find this expectation self-fulfilling. More importantly, where tutors are doubtful about their student's potential this will also be communicated and be self-fulfilling. This may seem a little far-fetched but there are several pieces of research confirming this phenomenon. It began with the original research by Rosenthall and Jacobson, reported in their book '*Pygmalian in the Classroom*'. They took two classes of mixed ability children: the teacher of Class A was told that all the children in this class were of high ability and the teacher of Class B was told that all the children in that class were of low ability. At the end of the year all children in Class A had higher attainments and all children in Class B had lower attainments. All the children had performed according to their teachers' expectations.

Tutors may sometimes have either a negative or a positive attitude towards their students' abilities which may not always be based on objective evidence. The main point about the expectancy effect is that it appears to be an unconscious process. Tutors may think that this is obvious enough but the research is persuasive in demonstrating how easy it is for us all to make false judgements about people on the slenderest of evidence. A common example is the tendency to judge a person's intelligence by their speech or their dress. However, if tutors are aware of this possibility it need not happen and they will be conscious of the need to be optimistic and encouraging at all times.

Seek the student's point of view

People who have low self-esteem are often reluctant to express an opinion. The tutor should try to encourage them to express opinions as this can have a very positive effect on self-esteem.

Their opinion could be sought, for instance, on a news topic of the day. Besides giving the student a feeling of worth, this technique can alse serve as an 'ice-breaker' with a student who may at first be feeling ill at ease.

There may be occasions when a student expresses values at variance to those of the tutor. In these circumstances it is important that the tutor does not argue the point. The student's right to have different opinions and values must be respected. However, this does not mean that the tutor should compromise their own position on the topic at issue. They should simply show interest and perhaps ask for the reasons for the different opinion.

Summary

Organising the programme

- Details of sessions will depend on the individual personality of the tutor.
- Tutors should meet students before the programme to explain procedures.
- The sessions should be organised in comfortable and private surroundings if possible.
- Tutors should explain to students the relationship between self-esteem and achievement.
- Students should be told that the sessions are private and so confidential.
- Tutors should inform their organiser if a student shows difficult behaviour.
- Tutors should make notes of the sessions after the student has left.

The ingredients of the sessions

- Listen to feelings as well as to words.
- Do not question directly; respect the student's need for privacy.
- Praise honestly where possible.
- Praise personality as well as achievement and effort.
- Seek the student's point of view on important topics.

- Emphasise positive expectancies.
- Do not confuse understanding with patronising.
- Try to empower the student; teach towards internal locus of control.
- Be prepared for both the quiet student and the talkative student.

Further reading

Devine, T. G. (1981) *Teaching Study Skills: Guide for Teachers*. Boston: Alleyn and Bacon.

Gittins, R. (1985) *An Introduction to Literacy Teaching*. London: Albsu Publications.

Lawrence, D. (1996) *Enhancing Self-esteem in the Classroom* (2nd edn). London: Paul Chapman.

Chapter 7

The Self-Esteem Enhancement Programme

Introduction

This chapter outlines a Self-Esteem Enhancement Programme of activities for the use of tutors who may wish to help students develop their self-esteem in a systematic way. It covers the development of social skills and other personal qualities considered to be essential in the growth towards positive self-worth. There are six sessions in the programme, which can be given in its entirety or in parts as the tutor thinks fit. Students who show extremely low self-esteem would probably benefit from the whole programme whilst for others it may be that they need to develop only specific skills. In the latter case, it would only be necessary to complete the session concerned with the particular skill in question. The programme is designed to be used with individual students or with groups of not more than six. The frequency of the sessions will, of course, depend on the exigencies of each service. It is suggested that for students who have shown interest in completing the full programme the self-esteem sessions be alternated with the usual sessions on skill tutoring and should last not more than one hour each.

Although this programme is designed for self-esteem enhancement, it cannot be sufficiently emphasised that it is the quality of the tutor–student relationship that is the key factor in any such programme. This is why the first part of the book focused primarily on the tutor getting to know the student and on the tutor's communication skills. For the programme outlined here to be effective it is essential first that the tutor is skilled in communication and is able to present to the student a high self-esteem model.

The tutor will recognise in the programme outlined here some of the social skills that were discussed in the first part of the book. The activities suggested to develop these skills are discussed in both parts simply because on occasions they can be useful to both student and tutor. Session 5 on coping with stress is an example of this. There is a reciprocal relationship between emotional stress, self-esteem and performance. When a student is under stress their self-esteem will be low and they will not achieve as much. When a tutor is under stresss, their self-esteem will also be low and they will not teach as efficiently. Session 4 on being assertive is another example of activities useful to both students and tutors. This again is because of a significant relationship between self-esteem and the ability to be assertive.

Session 1: Introducing the Self-Esteem Enhancement Programme to the student

Where the tutor has made the decision to follow this systematic programme of self-esteem enhancement the next step is to discuss its operation with the student. This should be done with some care and preparation. Obviously it would be quite a threat for the student to be informed by the tutor that they were about to 'develop their self-esteem'!

The way in which the programme should be introduced will vary with the individual as not all students will react in the same way. However, it is advisable to follow certain principles. First, explain to the student that people always learn best when they are confident and believe in themselves. Say that you wonder whether they might like to work through a programme designed to help develop confidence and that it has been found to be successful with other groups. Explain that this would be in addition to the normal sessions on improving literacy skills and that you would like to alternate the session on the teaching of literacy skills with one on the six-session Self-Esteem Enhancement Programme. Also explain that the self-esteem exercises they complete during the sessions would have to be practised at home during the forthcoming week to be really effective. The results of this 'homework' would then be discussed at the beginning of each of the sessions. Assuming that the student continues to show interest, the details of the programme can then be discussed. Should the student show any signs of unease about the plan it is best not to put any pressure at all on the student to engage in the programme. It would not work without their full co-operation and their desire to enhance their self-esteem. It must be emphasised here that in order for the programme to be successful participation in it must be voluntary. The remainder of this chapter is devoted to the programme.

Know thyself

After explaining the programme, tutors should explain to their students that they may find it helpful to learn a bit more about themselves before actually beginning the specific exercises.

Explain to the student that there are three questionnaires which research has shown to be useful in assessing three basic personal qualities in people. Then give the student the option of either doing them now with the tutor or else taking them away for completion at home before the next session. Whatever their decision, it is important that the tutor now explains each of the traits being measured and how to measure them, as illustrated below.

1. Self-esteem questionnaire

Self-esteem is really 'confidence' and has two aspects. It refers first to your confidence in yourself as a person and secondly to your confidence in your abilities. In order to measure this, a series of questions are presented to which the answers are either 'yes', 'no', or 'don't know'. Each answer in a positive direction is usually given a score and the sum total of these is considered to be the person's level of self-esteem.

Discuss the results of each question in turn, allowing the student to do the talking. Do not criticise the results but reassure where a low score is made that many people feel the same way. Conclude with positive comments, e.g. 'Now you know yourself a bit better you are in a strong position to change anything if you want to'.

The student self-esteem questionnaire

	Always	Sometimes	Never
1. Are there lots of things about yourself you do not like?			
2. Do you worry about things you should have done or said?			
3. Do you often lie awake at night worrying about things?			
4. Do you wish you were somebody else?			
5. Do you hate having to return faulty goods to a shop			
6. Do other people criticise you for what you say or do?			
7. Are you easily hurt when people find fault with you?			
8. Do you try to avoid meetings which might be difficult?			
9. Do you feel that not many people like you?			
10. Do you worry about your past mistakes?			
11. Do you give in easily in the face of difficulties?			
12. Do you dislike the sound of your voice?			
13. Are you ashamed of your background?			
14. Are you anxious when meeting a new person?			
15. Do you find you can't think clearly in conversations?			
16. Are you easily embarrassed?			
17. Would you take a drug to help you get through a meeting?			
18. Do you dislike your appearance?			
19. Are other people more popular than you?			
20. Do you find it hard to make up your mind?			

Scoring the questionnaire
Always = 0   Sometimes = 1 point   Never = 2 points
Scores between 0 and 20 = low self-esteem
Scores between 21 and 30 = average self-esteem
Scores between 31 and 40 = high self-esteem

2. Emotionality questionnaire

This questionnaire measures the extent to which a person experiences emotions. Explain that most people are average on this dimension, but that it seems some people tend to be overemotional whilst others appear to be relatively unemotional. Explain to the student that research has shown that we are all born with differences in emotional temperament and this stays with us for life. *Emotionality* is an inherited temperament. Explain that some people appear to be highly emotional and tend to overact emotionally in situations, and others tend to be unemotional and seem to be more placid. It is helpful for the student to know how they rate on this dimension so that they are able better to make allowances for their temperament. For instance, if inclined to be highly emotional, then they can be prepared for it and can take two steps backwards, as it were, when feeling highly emotional and place the situation in better perspective. Knowledge of this dimension of personality also sometimes helps to explain other people's reactions. We are all different!

The student emotionality questionnaire

	Always	Sometimes	Never
1. Do other people say that you are a moody person?			
2. Do you lie awake at nights worrying about things?			
3. Do you worry that you might develop a serious illness?			
4. Would you be easily upset if a salesperson was rude to you?			
5. Do you usually cry when witnessing a tender scene on TV?			
6. Do you usually cry if you see an animal hurt?			
7. Do you ever cry when listening to music?			
8. Do you easily become irritable with people?			
9. Do other people say you have a temper?			
10. Are you easily hurt if you are criticised?			

Scoring the questionnaire
Always = 2 points   Sometimes = 1 point   Never = 0

Scores between 0 and 5 = low emotionality
Scores between 6 and 12 = average emotionality
Scores between 13 and 20 = high emotionality

Give reassurance if an extreme score has been made and explain the advantages of high emotionality if necessary, e.g. such a person experiences more joys in life. Explain the value of knowing your place on this dimension, e.g. forewarned is to be forearmed.

3. Introvert/extravert questionnaire

Explain to the student that as with the emotionality dimension, the introvert or extravert characteristic appears to be inherited. A few people prefer quiet pursuits whilst another few prefer more noisy pursuits but, again as with the emotionality dimension, most people are along the mid-point.

The student introvert/extravert questionnaire

	Always	Sometimes	Never
1. Do you become bored easily?			
2. Would you be unhappy spending a whole day alone?			
3. Would you prefer to have dinner with lots of friends rather than one other?			
4. Do you like to talk to other people when out shopping?			
5. Do you like lively parties?			
6. Would you prefer to holiday with lots of people or just one other?			
7. Do you speak first when meeting new people?			
8. Do you enjoy talking to a large group of people?			
9. Would you prefer to order goods by mail rather than in person?			
10. Do you try to vary the kind of clothes you wear?			

Scoring the questionnaire
Always = 2 points   Sometimes = 1 point   Never = 0

Scores between 0 and 5 = markedly introverted
Scores between 6 and 15 = average
Scores between 16 and 20 = markedly extraverted

Again, reassure where an extreme score is made – there is no relation between any scores on this questionnaire and ill health.

A score should be considered in relation to the particular student's lifestyle.

Final thoughts on questionnaires
It should be explained to the students that no questionnaire is 100 per cent reliable and that these scores should be used as guides. The main value of the self-esteem questionnaire is that it gives the student a baseline from which they can aspire to improve. They should repeat the questionnaire at the end of the Self-Esteem Enhancement Programme. The main value of the two inherited dimensions of personality probably lies in raising awareness among students regarding individual differences. Temperamental differences like emotionality and introversion/extraversion explain why sometimes a person finds it difficult to get on with another person.

Session 2: Developing spontaneity and self-acceptance

Explain to the student that the high self-esteem person is usually able to be spontaneous and to express themselves without fear or anxiety. Other people are more likely to feel they can trust the person who is spontaneous. You know where you stand with a person who freely expresses themselves, even if you might not always approve of what they express! People who are spontaneous are able to relate to others directly on a human level without hiding behind their status. They are not afraid to reveal themselves as they really are. A person who is not spontaneous is likely to react to others in terms of their stereotypical role, so that they behave as the typical teacher, the typical policeman, or the typical psychologist. They behave in ways typical of their profession, which makes it impossible to get to know the 'real person'. In other words, they are hiding behind their 'professional mask'. This is usually an automatic learned process but it can also be a defence against revealing their true selves. This is particularly the case where a person has a fear of being disliked or of being ridiculed. It is understandable that some students with literacy difficulties try to minimise their literacy problems and sometimes even deny them, especially when in public. Hiding behind their 'persona' is for them a way of protecting their self-esteem. Where this happens, tutors should aim to help these students face the fact that they have literacy difficulties – in order to enhance self-esteem it is first essential that people have a realistic self-image.

Spontaneity

Explain to the student that in this session they are shown how to practise being spontaneous.

Exercise 1 for groups

Students in turn are asked to pick out a piece of paper from a bag. A particular emotion is written on each piece of paper. The student has to act out the emotion while the rest of the group guess what it is. The following emotions are written by the tutor on the paper:

anger
joy
embarrassement
fear
curiosity
tranquillity

Exercise 2 for individuals or groups

Each student is asked 'Who are you?' After the reply the question is asked again and this procedure is repeated four times. Most people would reply at first with their names, and then perhaps say whether they are married, or a father, or a mother, and then would be likely to give their job or profession. It is not unusual to meet resistance at first. Where this happens: e.g. 'I can't think of anything', support the student with a personal trait, 'But I know that you are a kind person'. Do not persist where a student becomes unduly embarrassed.

Exercise 3 for groups

Students are asked to complete the following sentences aloud:

- I like it when . . .
- I dislike it when . . .
- I am proud of . . .
- I am afraid of . . .

- I become embarrassed when . . .
- I am happy when . . .

Again, no pressure should be put on a student who is clearly having difficulty completing a sentence. Do praise for courage in being able to reveal themselves.

Self-acceptance

On completion of the exercises the tutor should read the following passage to the students and then discuss it with them:

'A high self-esteem person is spontaneous and is also "self-accepting". That is, they do not reject, or hide, who they are. These people are able to value themselves, even if they do not always like what they do or perhaps even like their behaviour. They believe in their potential to change. They are able to take an objective attitude towards any apparent inadequacy and not let it affect their whole personality. So a student with literacy difficulties should adopt the attitude that they can change and eventually they will be able to improve their literacy difficulties. Also, having literacy difficulties is only one part of their personality. There are probably other parts to their personality that they and other people like and value. The adoption of this positive attitude will prevent any negative feelings about literacy difficulties generalising to the whole personality and so prevent feeling inadequate as a person generally.'

This positive attitude of valuing self should be encouraged by tutors at regular intervals throughout the course.

Discussion
- Why do some people find it hard to say what they really want to say?
- Do some people feel this is because they might be rejected or disliked?
- What makes us trust some people and not others?
- How does it feel to be able to express ourselves freely without fear?
- Can we accept some bad things about ourselves without feeling inadequate generally?

Homework

1. When next the students meet an acquaintance or a stranger they should make a point of revealing something of themselves in conservation by giving an opinion, e.g. 'This weather is awful. I feel really cold today'.
2. When purchasing an article in a shop students should deliberately make some comment about the article, e.g. 'This is a very popular one, I believe'.
3. Students should seek out a friend or relative and give an opinion on the latest news item or a television programme.
4. Students should prepare a written statement of their opinion on a news item of their choice and bring this to the next session with their tutor.

Summary

- High self-esteem people are usually spontaneous and able to express their 'real selves'.
- People trust best those whom they feel to be expressing their 'real selves'.
- People who can be spontaneous are better communicators.
- People can learn how to be more spontaneous.
- High self-esteem people accept and value themselves if not their behaviour.
- High self-esteem people believe in their potential to change.

Session 3: Looking the part – body language

The following should be read to the students and then discussed:

'One of the most fascinating areas of modern psychology has been the research into non-verbal behaviour more commonly known as "body language". It is a fact that people react to one another not only in terms of what they say but also in terms of what they look like and sound like. This is particularly the case on first meeting somebody. Almost as soon as you meet another person you begin the process of trying to decide what kind of person they are – whether you like them – what age they are – what they do for a living, etc. This is done almost automatically and even if there are no real clues on which to work people will still make assumptions based on body language. It seems that nature abhors a vacuum so people have need to make sense or to structure a situation so they know where they stand. Judgements are often made on the slenderest of evidence. More often than not, it is the person's bearing, their clothes, their voice which are the first things people are aware of, and not what is said.

'There has been much research over the years into the nature of "body language". Most people are aware of the work of the anthropologists who have shown us that we often communicate unconsciously, in primitive fashion, through body language. It seems that we have retained many of the patterns of communication seen in the animal world. Every time we speak we send messages through our facial expression, hand gestures, tone of voice, body posture and eye contact. It is as if our body reflects our feelings. The social psychologists have shown how these feelings are expressed quite unconsciously in this way. This means that it is not easy to say one thing and mean another without our body giving the game away. There are some people, however, who are able to disguise their real feelings by deliberately putting on an act. Obviously, some are better at this than others, and for most of us our body language reflects our verbal message.

'Although our body language seems to accompany our verbal messages in an instinctive way and so is generally outside our control, it is possible to become aware of our non-verbal behaviour and so be able to change it. This is what happens when some people are able to tell untruths 'without batting an eyelid', as they say.

'High self-esteem people generally look confident; their body language gives a confident impression. Their body stance and facial expressions are relaxed; their voice tone is calm and well-modulated; they look you in the eye when talking to you. Low self-esteem people generally give the opposite impression, communicating a general air of tenseness. Clearly, it is important for low self-esteem people to try to present a more confident model of themselves.

'Research psychologists have demonstrated how people can learn through practice how to do this. Even more important is the discovery that people who deliberately adopt a confident stance, learn how to relax and how to modulate their voice tone, begin to feel more confident. Not only does body language reflect the verbal message but our feelings reflect our body language to some extent. To feel confident act confident!'

Discussion
- What is body language?
- How do people communicate through body language?
- Do body language and verbal messages always say the same things?
- How can we change our body language to look confident?

Exercises
The following exercises are designed first to help students become aware of possible negative aspects of their body language, and second to help students learn how to change them.

Exercise 1: Students work in triads. A talks to B for two minutes about a hobby. C observes and records the non-verbal behaviour of both on the checklist below. Results are discussed and roles changed. The procedure is repeated until all three have had a turn at being the observer.

	A		B	
	Relaxed	*Tense*	*Relaxed*	*Tense*
Arms				
Shoulders				
Legs				
Torso				
Face				
Hands				
Neck				
Voice				

Exercise 2: Again working in triads, student A reads to B the text below while C observes and records the behaviour again on the checklist. Ensure all receive a turn at being A.

A Good morning! I am calling to ask if you would like to buy a copy of the latest magazine on motor cycle maintenance. I noticed that you have a motor bike leaning against your garage wall. Is it yours?

B I do not want to buy a copy of the motor bike magazine and the bike you saw has nothing to do with me. Goodbye!

A Ah! but you haven't seen it yet. This is not just about motor bikes; it covers all kinds of outside interests, including camping, walking and sailing. Surely you are interested in one of those.

B No! and would you please go away.

A Certainly I'll go but first I must let you see a copy so you can see just what you will be missing. This is the best magazine on the bookstalls.

Homework

Students are asked to notice, when next in a public place, e.g. on a bus, in a café, in a pub, or at work, how people are using eye contact when they converse. Watch to see if they break eye contact at all and at what point in a conversation. In normal conversation it is usual to look away from time to time in an easy way. Normal eye contact does not mean a fixed stare!

Summary

- High self-esteem people look confident.
- Being confident means looking relaxed.
- Being relaxed means feeling confident.
- People can learn to look confident.

Session 4: Being assertive

The following should be read to the students and then discussed:

'People who are assertive have no trouble in making their needs known. They are usually of high self-esteem and so are spontaneous and able to express themselves without fear. This does not mean that they are aggressive. Aggression and assertion are two different things. People who are aggressive are rude and unpleasant. People who are assertive are also expressing their needs, but in a pleasant way. People who are submissive express their needs through being subservient and humble. Being an assertive person does not mean being a selfish person. Unless your own needs are expressed freely you end up feeling frustrated and you are not then going to be in a position unselfishly to satisfy other people's needs. In other words "charity begins at home".'

The following table illustrates the differences between these three modes of expression.

Aggressive	Assertive	Submissive
rude	polite	humble
unpleasant	pleasant	servile
arrogant	confident	timid

The three different ways of expressing needs can be plotted along a continuum with aggressive behaviour at one end and submissive behaviour at the other end. The continuum is illustrated in the following exercise.

Exercise 1
It can be seen in this exercise that assertive behaviour lies in the middle of a continuum. Students are asked to rate themselves on the continuum by placing a cross on the number that they believe best represents themselves. Colleagues who know them are then asked to do the same. They should discuss the results.

Aggressive				Assertive			Submissive		
1	2	3	4	5	6	7	8	9	10

Using the right words

Thomas Gordon, a famous American psychologist, advocates a method of resolving conflicts by using the right words. These words are 'I' – 'when' – 'because'.

- 'I' is used first to express directly your feelings about the topic.
- 'When' is used to describe the behaviour.
- 'Because' is used to give a rational reason.

The following sentence illustrates the use of these three words:

'I feel upset when you use my pen without asking permission because I need it myself.'

Exercise 2

Students are asked to insert phrases under the listed headings to illustrate the use of the three words 'I' – 'when' – 'because'. The first one is done as an example.

Scene	Behaviour	Feeling	Reason
1. Friend borrows my new bike without asking my permission	'When you borrowed my bike without asking permission . . .	I felt upset . . .	because I needed it myself urgently.'
2. A fellow student regularly spills coffee on your desk			
3. A friend regularly asks you to pick up books for them in the library			
4. A colleague always borrows your pencils rather than buys their own			

If this exercise is completed correctly using the three words described, the person concerned is demonstrating assertive behaviour and does not sound aggressive. An aggressive person with low self-esteem might have used 'you' messages and been unpleasantly personal: 'You are always borrowing my things and I don't like it!'

The three recommended words are used for the following reasons:

- 'I' is used so that feelings are immediately expressed.
- 'When' is used as it implies that it is only under those particular circumstances that the feelings apply and not for ever more. This means that the person has a chance to reform!
- 'Because' is used to give a rational explanation for the comments, communicating that this is not merely an emotional outburst.

Exercise 3

In addition to using the three words as described above, a conflict situation sometimes demands the use of the 'broken record' technique. This means repeating a request quietly, perhaps several times if it is refused the first time. The following scene illustrates this and also the use of the three words. It should be enacted by two students, with an audience followed by discussion.

Scene: A student is returning a pair of trousers to a shop because on arriving home they were found to be the wrong size. The student had asked for a size 30 but they were found to be a 32.

Assistant Hello again! How can I help you this time?

Student I am returning these trousers as they are the wrong size. They are size 32. I needed a 30.

Assistant What do you mean? I checked the size before you left the shop and it was a 30.

Student There must have been a mistake as they are definitely a size 32.

Assistant But I don't have a size 30.

Student OK, then I would like a refund please.

Assistant We don't give refunds. You'll just have to have a credit note.

Student No thanks. I would like my money back please.

Assistant I cannot give a refund.

Student I would like my money back please. (broken record)

Assistant I've told you already you can have a credit note but no refund.

Student (feeling angry but determined not to be aggressive) When you say that to me I feel upset because I know it is the law to give refunds under these circumstances.

Assistant (becoming angry) Who do you think you are to tell me what to do!

Student I would like my money back please so bring the manager.

Assistant How about taking something else from the shop instead of trousers?

Student No thanks, I want my money back.

Assistant Well you can't have it!

Student   If that's the case I'll just have to take legal advice because when you talk to me like that I feel angry.
Assistant (angry) Oh! here's your money.

This conversation may sound a bit artificial and in a real life
situation the details will vary according to the circumstances.
However, the main principles of using the 'broken record' technique together with the use of the three recommended words
and the avoidance of 'you' messages would still apply.

Analysing a situation which requires assertion

It is possible to think of any behaviour under three categories –
feelings, action and **thinking**. These aspects of behaviour all
affect each other so that if we change one of them we change the
other two also. To develop assertive behaviour you need to be
aware of your reactions under these three headings of feelings,
action and thinking.

Exercise 4
This exercise shows you how to analyse your behaviour in this
way. Two examples are presented. The first is an analysis of the
behaviour of an unassertive person, the second is an analysis of
the behaviour of an assertive person.

Scene: You are next to be served in a shop but the shop assistant
ignores you and serves another.

Example 1	*feelings*	anger, humiliation, embarrassment.
	thinking	'I must be insignificant. What a rude person!'
	action	Leave the shop in anger muttering quietly, 'You are a very rude person!'
Example 2	*feelings*	irritation.
	thinking	'This is an incompetent shop assistant. I'll have to tell him I am next to be served.'
	action	'Excuse me but I am next to be served.'

In the unnassertive example the situation was taken personally
and submissively. In the second scene the assertive person did

not take the ignoring personally but viewed it logically. Note also the use of 'I' and that there was no reference to the shop assistant's incompetence as was the case in the unassertive example.

Homework

1. Students are asked to write out the words they might use when being asked by a beggar to give them money and responding assertively.
2. Students write out words to use in the same situation, responding aggressively.
3. Students write out words to use in the same situation, responding submissively.

Summary

People usually express their needs to others in one of three different ways:

1. Through being aggressive (not recommended).
2. Through being submissive (not recommended).
3. Through being assertive (recommended).

The assertive person would use the three words 'I' – 'When' – 'Because' in a conflict situation. In addition, the 'broken record' technique may also have to be used.

Session 5: Coping with stress

Stress is a fashionable word in today's society and most people confess to having been under stress at some time or another. The symptoms people describe as 'stress', however, are probably as varied as the number of people experiencing it. For one person it can mean being totally incapacitated while another may describe it as merely feeling 'under the weather'. Some stress is serious and surveys have revealed that people who regularly visit their GP, for instance, usually have a stress-related illness. A definition for our purposes would be a feeling of psychological pressure with some adverse bodily accompaniment. For example, a student who is confronted with a forthcoming examination knowing that they are likely to do badly, perhaps as a result of poor spelling, may be having sleepless nights over it. Eventually, they become exhausted; an initial psychological stimulus has resulted in a physical condition. Like most psychological concepts, there are degrees. For some it can involve raised blood pressure, irregular heart rhythm, butterflies in the stomach and breathing difficulties, whereas for the next person it may simply be a feeling of frustration accompanied by a mild headache. The particular reaction will be determined by two things – the severity of the events themselves and the person's capacity to tolerate frustration. While often we can do nothing about certain events we can all do something about our capacity to tolerate frustration. In other words, we can increase our coping capacities. In this session students are shown how to practise strategies so that they are able eventually to minimise the effects of potentially stress-provoking events and also become better able to handle other types of stress which sometimes strike us all without warning.

It is suggested that the tutor begin the session by talking about stress as referred to above and then presenting students with the following questions as a basis for discussion:

- What do we mean by stress?
- What causes stress?
- How should we cope with stress?

Following the discussion, students should be asked to complete the questionnaire on page 85. This activity should be followed by a discussion on the results, with tutors remembering to be empathic and non-critical. The giving of advice should be resisted.

Minimising stress

Everybody is capable at some stage of developing stress symptoms. It is possible, however, to go some way towards reducing the chances of developing stress by following a particular regime. This involves caring for yourself and in effect being your

Stress questionnaire

	Yes	Don't know	No
1. Do you feel irritable or bad tempered most of the time?			
2. Do you have difficulty accepting any kind of criticism?			
3. Do you find that you rarely laugh at anything?			
4. Do you worry over not meeting deadlines?			
5. Is there somebody you just cannot get on with?			
6. Can you say 'No' to other people when you want to?			
7. Are you living the kind of life you choose to live?			
8. Do you feel 'taken for granted' by anybody?			
9. Do you often wake in the night thinking about some problem?			
10. Are you always worrying over having to balance your finances?			
11. Are you able to engage regularly in some hobby or leisure pursuit?			
12. Are you able to take regular physical exercise?			
13. Are you always worrying about things that might happen?			
14. Would you find difficulty in sitting in a chair and doing nothing?			
15. Are you finding that you are drinking and/or smoking too much?			
16. Do you find it easy to get off to sleep at nights?			

Scoring the questionnaire
2 points if the answer is YES to the following: 1, 2, 3, 4, 5, 8, 9, 10, 13, 14, 15
2 points if the answer is NO to the following: 6, 7, 11, 12, 16
1 point for every question answered DON'T KNOW

The higher the score the higher the stress level.

own counsellor. So even those students who appear not to have any symptoms of stress should try to follow this regime:

- Take regular time out for a leisure activity, e.g. reading, sport, socialising.

- Try to avoid the company of people known to be stressed and anxious.
- Learn to say 'No' when people make inappropriate demands on you.
- Practise assertiveness techniques.
- Delegate work where possible, even in the home.
- Listen to your body and rest if tired – nobody's energies are limitless.
- Take regular exercise to help release endorphins in the brain conducive to relaxation.
- Drink and eat in moderation allowing at least two days a week without alcohol.
- Try to see the funny side of things – stress is incompatible with a sense of humour.
- Put five minutes aside during the day for doing nothing except meditation or thinking.
- Learn a relaxation technique and practise it each day.
- Learn how to rid yourself of disruptive emotions using the Rational-Emotive Therapy.

The last two points on this list are explained in the following sections.

A relaxation procedure

First of all, there are many different kinds of relaxation techniques published and if the student has a favourite one they should continue to use it. If not, then the method outlined below should be used.

This relaxation procedure emphasises natural breathing. Natural breathing is automatic and normally outside conscious control. Unfortunately, when stressed we often force our breathing and there are even those who advocate consciously taking deep breaths. The method illustrated below consists of two stages. In Stage 1, relaxing the body, emphasis is placed on ensuring complete physical relaxation before observing the natural breathing. Once this has been achieved the word 'relax' is introduced and gradually associated with the relaxation process. Stage 2 comes once the body is relaxed. Positive affirmations are introduced, e.g. 'I am a relaxed person – I am a happy person – I have no worries', etc. The principles are as follows:

- Whenever two things regularly occur together the appearance of one will remind us of the other.
- The word 'relax' is regularly paired with the experience of physical relaxation.
- Eventually, merely saying the word 'relax' will cause the body to physically relax.
- In the real life situation, whenever feeling tense, quietly say 'relax' and the body will automatically be prompted to relax.
- With the body relaxed, positive thoughts can be introduced to enhance relaxation.

Stage 1 – Relaxing the body:

Find a comfortable chair. Ensure the chair properly supports the head

Remove shoes and sit comfortably, working through the following stages

Raise the eyes (not the head) to the ceiling and focus on a point above eye level

As the eyes become fatigued they can be closed

Think of the toes and wriggle them

Think of the ankle joints and relax them

Think of the calf muscles and relax them

Think of the knee joints and relax them

Think of the thigh muscles and relax them

Working up the sides of the body think about relaxing all muscles

Think of the shoulder muscles and relax them

Work along the back of the neck relaxing the neck muscles

Work up the back of the head and down the face relaxing as you go

Let the jaw drop and even the tongue in the mouth should relax

Work down the chest relaxing all muscles as you go

Focus on the stomach muscles and relax them

Think now of the breathing – observe it – it is automatic – don't force it

Let 'it' breathe in and out when 'it' wants to

After every breath out say the word 'relax'
Repeat the word after every breath for ten times taking as
long as 'it' wants.

Stage 2 – Positive affirmations:

Once the body is relaxed, positive affirmations, as below, are
introduced to reinforce the relaxation. This is very like self-
hypnosis and can be a powerful method if practised regularly.

I am a relaxed person
I am a happy person
I have no worries
I like myself
I am a confident person

Other positive affirmations can be introduced as appropriate.

Rational-Emotive Therapy

In Chapter 5 on developing the skills, Rational-Emotive Therapy
was outlined as a method of increasing confidence. This method
would also lend itself to helping the brighter students who may
be suffering stress. So this section is designed specifically for
students. The topic could be introduced to students as follows:

The main principle of RET is that events in themselves do not
cause our emotions. We all have a tendency to say things like
'He makes me so angry', when in fact we make ourselves angry.
It is not the other person who makes us feel angry, but rather it
is our interpretation of the event which produces the anger
within us. In other words, it is thinking which causes emotion,
not events. So if you have an argument with another student try
to take two steps backwards before reacting and remember that
you are responsible for your own feelings and analyse your
thinking. Ask yourself what you were thinking at the time. As
an example, let's say you are upset because your partner has left
you. The tendency is to blame yourself for your misery. Now if
you stopped to analyse your thinking you will probably discover that you had unspoken thoughts that are not rational, such
as 'I must be a horrible person. I'll never find another partner

like that'. The next step in this analysis is to challenge or dispute this thinking. The aim in this step is to unravel rational from irrational thinking, because so often our thinking is irrational in these circumstances, and it is the irrational thinking that so often causes us pain. During this step you have to be a scientist in effect and ask yourself 'Where is the evidence . . .?' you should ask yourself 'Where is the evidence that I am a horrible person?' The answer, of course, is that this is irrational and there is no evidence. In fact, there must be lots of other people who do not think you are horrible. So that thought has to be dismissed and substituted for positive ones, e.g. 'There is no evidence that I am horrible. There is a good chance that I am an attractive person otherwise I would not have had this partner in the first place. Also there is no evidence that I won't find another partner'. You are now taking a scientific attitude and asking always for the evidence. This does not mean that your feelings of misery will immediately disappear, but it does mean they are likely to be watered down. The chart illustrates what can happen when feelings are watered down or reduced in this way.

The feeling	Strong	Moderate	Mild
anger	furious	angry	annoyed
fear	terrified	anxious	concerned
sadness	miserable	depressed	blue
hurt	crushed	let down	disappointed
shame	humiliated	embarrassed	uncomfortable

The next step therefore, after changing the thinking, is to deliberately try to reduce the intensity of the feeling by considering the milder alternatives. This method of analysing behaviour is known as the ABCDE method. The example given above would be analysed as follows:

A = activating event – partner leaves for another
B = belief about the event – irrational thoughts
C = consequences – feelings of misery and humiliation
D = disputing the thinking – exchanging irrational for rational thoughts
E = effects after disputing the thoughts – pleasanter emotions

For a fuller account of Rational-Emotive Therapy you should refer to the original works of Ellis. For the purpose of being able to minimise stress the above simplified account should prove adequate. Like most things worth having, it does require some effort and in this case the main effort lies in practising disputing your thinking – changing irrational to rational thoughts.

Exercise
Students are asked to describe an event that they perceive as stressful. This could be something they have experienced in the past. If they cannot, or do not wish to recall the event, suggest the following: *You cannot enter the classroom without feeling sick.* Students are asked to analyse the event using the ABCDE classification. Tutor gives assistance, particularly by helping dispute negative thoughts. Students are encouraged to substitute negative thoughts with positive ones. Students then do the relaxation procedure as outlined earlier, introducing the new positive thoughts.

The following is a possible analysis of this hypothetical situation:

A = Activating event	*B = Belief*	*C = Consequences*
Cannot enter class without feeling sick	'I am stupid. I'll never be able to do this course.'	Feelings of humiliation, anxiety, shame.

D = Disputation	*E = Effect*
'How does being afraid to enter a classroom mean I am stupid? I can do lots of other things so I can't be stupid.'	'I may feel uneasy at entering the classroom but I can do it with practice. I like myself really.'

Homework

Students are asked to practise the relaxation technique outlined earlier in this session.

Summary

- We are all capable of experiencing stress symptoms.
- Stress begins with a psychological feeling but ends with physical symptoms.

- We can learn techniques to minimise the effects of stress.
- The Rational-Emotive approach is a useful technique.
- There are hints on avoiding stress that can be learned.

Session 6: Strengthening the Self

In the first four sessions of the Self-Esteem Enhancement Programme the emphasis was on enhancing self-esteem through developing specific personal qualities. In Session 5, on coping with stress, the emphasis changed from learning skills to showing students how to protect themselves from events that can cause stress. This is because the experience of stress usually results in a lowering of self-esteem.

The theme of showing students how to protect themselves is taken further in this session. Students are shown how to use 'psychological innoculation' against stress by using appropriate strategies to strengthen and value the Self.

In our kind of culture, people who talk of their achievements or of their talents are often called conceited or else are thought to be eccentric. These people are unpopular and often regarded with suspicion. They are also described as self-centred and boastful. Modesty is valued and society appears to put pressure on people to be modest. This is seen particularly in the media where a sporting hero or a movie star, for instance, becomes heady with their achievements and is then targeted as needing to be 'brought down a peg or two'. This attitude is so prevalent that it even has its own name and has become known as the 'tall poppy syndrome'. People who are considered to be 'tall poppies' are thought to be in need of cutting down and are said to have become 'above themselves'.

As a result of this kind of pressure in society people often seem to be afraid even to refer to their talents and this has produced another kind of person who is just as unpopular – the one who is self-depreciating to the extreme. These people behave as if they have no self-worth at all.

From the point of view of building self-esteem, both these extreme attitudes are undesirable. People with low self-esteem are inclined to express this in the two extreme ways described. If they are extraverted in temperament they will be more likely to be boastful in an attempt to compensate for inadequacies. In contrast, people of introverted temperament will be more likely to express their low self-esteem by being diffident and self-depreciating.

People of high self-esteem are quietly aware of their own self-worth. They do not feel the need to boast but neither do they feel the need to minimise their achievements. Even where they may have an inadequacy, they do not let it generalise to the whole personality.

In this session students are encouraged to value themselves by discussing their talents and giving each other the experience of positive feedback.

Positive feedback

Exercise 1

1. Students sit in a circle facing each other. One is designated the 'Angel' while the others take turns in giving the Angel a compliment. That rule is that they have 60 seconds in which to do this or else they are 'out'. Another rule is that nobody must give a 'put down' or else they are 'out'. After having gone around the circle the person on the left of the Angel takes over the role. The same procedure occurs and continues until everybody has had a turn at being the Angel.

2. After completion of the exercise, discuss how students felt when they received the compliments. Why do they think that they felt embarrassed, for instance? Reference can then be made to the points made in the introduction to the session, particularly regarding society's pressure on people to be modest.

Exercise 2

1. Students are asked to make a list of their positive qualities. Tutors may need to give some assistance with this, e.g. helpful, courageous, kind, etc. When students have listed at least four qualities, they are asked to read them out aloud to the group in turn. Prior instructions are given to the group that nobody must criticise or comment unfavourably on the readings.

2. This exercise should be followed again by a discussion on how it felt to be complimenting themselves in public in this way.

Conditioning the unconscious mind

The mind consists of both conscious and unconscious thoughts. It has been likened to an iceberg, with two-thirds of it below the surface (see Figure 6). As such, it consists of three layers. The first layer is the part that is **conscious** and contains our present thoughts and feelings. The second layer is the part that is just below the surface, sometimes called the **subconscious**, and contains memories and feelings that can easily be recalled with questioning, e.g. 'What did you have for breakfast?' The third layer is usually known as the **unconscious** and contains long-forgotten memories. However, the mind can also be likened to a computer, with nothing ever truly forgotten, so that these apparently forgotten memories are still there. The evidence for this comes from hypnosis and also from dreams.

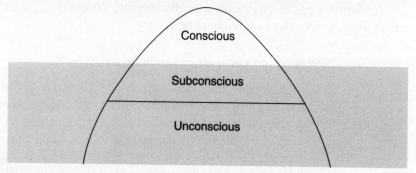

Figure 6   The structure of the mind

Exercise 3
In this exercise students are asked to use the relaxation procedure illustrated in the previous session on stress, and then to repeat affirmations which have been designed to strengthen the Self. This procedure is sometimes known as creative visualisation and is recommended as a method of changing negative feelings to positive ones. The act of total relaxation, or meditation, results in a state of mind that has often been referred to as 'tapping the unconscious'. It is hypothesised that the act of

imagining and 'seeing' oneself in a relaxing scene is imprinted on the unconscious mind.

> Once you are feeling perfectly relaxed think of a scene where you are always happy and content, or where you have been happy and content in the past.
> Concentrate on this scene for about two minutes recapturing the emotions you felt at the time.
> Now recall another experience, one where you behaved badly or without confidence and which still troubles you.
> See yourself in this scene but quickly change it so that you see yourself behaving properly and confidently this time.
> Now say to yourself the following affirmations: 'I am a confident person. I am a happy person. I like myself. Other people like me too. I have no worries.'

It is important that you visualise scenes while doing this exercise as the unconscious mind operates in pictures. Dreams are an example of this. Merely repeating the affirmations is not enough to produce a change. It is not enough just to keep repeating 'I am a confident person' without actually seeing yourself in your imagination actually behaving confidently.

Being responsible for my own behaviour

In Chapter 5 on developing the skills, reference was made to the concept of 'locus of control'. Some people find it difficult to take responsibility for themselves and are always blaming others for their predicaments. The behaviour of other people is a favourite excuse for their own deficiencies or weaknesses. Perhaps the influence of psychoanalysis has something to do with this attitude as it is not uncommon to hear a person blame their childhood. Most people these days have heard of Freud and his theories relating to childhood. One of his basic theories was that personality is determined by our childhood experiences and in order to become healthy adults we may need to unravel any unfortunate childhood experiences before moving on. We now know this to be erroneous. We are certainly influenced by our childhood experiences, together with our inherited traits, but it is not necessary to delve into the past in order to change any undesirable qualities in ourselves. We can start with the 'here and now' as human beings are motivated by the future if they allow themselves to be so. It is more important to know where we are going rather than where we have been when it comes to resolving any personality weaknesses.

Students who may show concern over certain aspects of their personalities need to be aware of this. In order to develop high self-esteem they need to adopt this new attitude of belief in the power to change by focusing on the present.

Exercise 4

This consists of a discussion with students on the theme of how far people are influenced by their personal histories. The following questions should be addressed:

- What possible events in a person's early life could still affect them as adults?
- What events in our present lives could contribute to our happiness?
- Are we all completely responsible for our own behaviour?
- How could we change things in ourselves we do not like?

Homework

1. Students are asked to draw up a 'life line'. This is a drawn line along which they place events of significance that have occurred in their lives to date. An example is given below:

2 yrs	5 yrs	15 yrs	20 yrs	30 yrs
baby brother born	started school	first girl friend	parents separated	married

2. Students should prepare answers to the following questions for discussion at the next session.

- Can you recall the emotions you experienced at the time of the significant events?
- Do you feel different now?
- If the same things occurred now would you do anything different?
- Do you feel that some events are still affecting you and if so, how?
- What can you do in order to prevent past events having an effect in the present?

Chapter 8

Developing a positive lifestyle

In the first chapter of this book we discussed how people who fail in an important area of their lives tend to feel failures generally. The Self-Esteem Enhancement Programme has tried to show that students with literacy difficulties do not necessarily need to lose confidence and demonstrate low self-esteem even though they may not yet have achieved a functional level of literacy. In this final chapter emphasis is placed on the need for a particular philosophy and a positive lifestyle as a further step towards maintaining self-esteem; it applies to both students and tutors.

Most people would agree that a major goal in life is the achievement of happiness. Unfortunately, it is difficult to set out consciously to achieve happiness. It is something that you either have or you don't. It seems to be a consequence of the manner in which you conduct your life in general. In other words, it is a by-product of living. The confident, high self-esteem person is usually a happy person and has formulated a personal philosophy of what life is all about. For some this is a religious philosophy, although it need not be so. It seems that a major goal in life is the seeking of pleasure and the avoidance of pain, not only for ourselves but also for other people. Albert Ellis, referred to in the session on stress, calls this 'responsible hedonism'. It does not mean seeking pleasure for its own sake but rather seeking pleasure which has no side-effects of pain, either to oneself or to others. For example, excessive alcohol consumption may be pleasurable in the short term but can have long-term undesirable consequences. Responsible hedonism implies the adoption of a caring, sharing attitude towards others as well as towards oneself.

It can be a salutary experience for most people to ask themselves if indeed they do have a philosophy of life. Some may find this an easy question to answer but for many it will be difficult and a new exercise in introspection. The following principles are suggested for consideration by both students and tutors as a possible means towards this philosophy of responsible hedonism.

Setting goals

The first of these principles is the need to set goals. This is important not just for the development of confidence; it is important in any area of mental health. It is the natural state of the human psyche to be motivated towards the future. Also, the human psyche, in its naturally healthy state, is always active in the same way as physiologically the nerve impulse is always active. The ideal state for the human being is not one of lying on a tropical beach somewhere for weeks on end, totally inactive, attractive as this may seem. The normal healthy state is to be planning for and moving towards some goal. Goals do not have to be dramatic, like sailing around the world single-handed – it could be the simple one of planning to plant flowers in the garden. But they do have to be realistic goals and have a definite purpose.

Some people worry because although they have goals they are unable to settle to them. They do not seem to lack energy but they tend to flit from one task to another and to procrastinate. There are two possible reasons for this. The first is that the goal may be too far away – as with the student who has not yet been able to begin to read or write but has a goal of completing a university degree. This illustrates the need for realistic goals and also for intermediate goals. In the example given the student should begin with the intermediate goal of completing a basic English course. The second reason for some people not being able to settle to their goals is because the goals may not be specific enough. They may have the admirable goal of achieving another academic qualification but have no definite plan or timescale for doing so.

In summary, goals have to be realistic and specific, and may need to be placed into two categories – intermediate and long term. It is not enough to have vague ideas of what you want to do. Goals have to be planned and to be realistic. A good plan is to sit down and make a list of the main areas of interest in your life and to enter a definite goal beside each one. Generally these will be long-term goals. In addition, you should have short-term goals for the day ahead. It is recommended that you begin each day before you get out of bed by saying to yourself, 'Plan for the day!' Then you know what lies ahead and this knowledge will give you a comfortable feeling.

Developing your skills

The learning of a new skill or the further development of an old one are sure confidence boosters. The knowledge that you are able to perform well at a chosen activity or that you are able to master a particular skill gives a feeling of confidence which can generalise to the whole personality. This is particularly the case if the skill is one that is valued by the people in your life whom you care about, or one that is valued by society in general. Psychotherapeutic programmes for the rehabilitation of the mentally ill often include the learning of a new skill for this reason.

Examples on record include the man who had been afraid to meet people because of imagined inferiority. He quickly overcame his problem once he had learned to play tennis. Children who learn to swim seem to gain in confidence overnight. The skill learned need not, of course, be a physical one. Confidence will come just as quickly, as outlined in the previous chapters, from learning how to develop personal skills in general.

Becoming an expert

It is an inescapable truth that the world needs experts. Whether this is a reflection of the kind of world we live in or a natural human need is debatable, but people seems to want to believe in experts. The expert is admired and revered. So if you are able to develop a talent in some direction and it becomes known to others it usually has the effect of enhancing your self-esteem and so increasing your level of confidence. The fascinating thing is that in order for this to happen you do not need to be an expert in the true sense of the word. The need for people to believe in experts is so widespread that merely the fact of being able to do something which others around you cannot do is enough to attract admiration. Even just showing interest in a particular topic and talking about it can have the same effect. If this is a topic the other person knows nothing about they will assume you know even more about it than you actually do and give you respect. It is easy to acquire a reputation in this way. The interesting thing is that when other people give you this respect for being, as they think, an expert, this in turn is motivating and usually has the effect of causing you to find out more on the subject, so before long you do actually become an expert!

Having fun

Life can be very serious indeed as most of us find out sooner or later. There are many reasons for this and there are times when most of us find ourselves taking a serious view of life; indeed often it is appropriate that we do so. It is hard not to be serious when you have a problem and for the person who lacks confidence life is rarely humorous. Lacking confidence is a serious matter. However, it is important to separate their confidence problem from their attitude to life in general. This means making a conscious effort to set out to have fun! Having fun is a characteristic of all living creatures. This is more in evidence during the early years of life, but the need to play remains dormant in all of us throughout life. Most people channel this into some kind of sport or recreation as adults and many of us retain a sense of fun from childhood which gives expression in everyday life.

The main point is that it seems to be human nature to want to play but this need can so easily be repressed, especially as we go through life and encounter various problems. This is what tends to happen to those who lack confidence. So when considering your lifestyle and whether it is conducive to happiness, ask yourself what you do to have fun. If the answer is nothing then it is imperative that you do something about it. Try to enagage your partner or a good friend in a search for regular recreation where you can let your hair down. Physical activities are ideal for this but not all of us are physically inclined. For other people even a visit to the cinema now and again could be a suitable alternative. It does not matter what pursuit you choose so long as it is geared to fun and it is one with which you feel comfortable. Also, try to see that there is often a funny side to life; even your own lack of confidence can be funny if you adopt the right attitude. The secret is to use the 'self-talk' described earlier and say to yourself, 'I do have a funny face when I am worried'. This can often do the trick and cause you to relax. A famous philosopher once said that a mark of the mature person is an ability to laugh at yourself. This is a true sense of humour. And above all never hold back laughter. If you feel like laughing do so even if you think it may not be approved of. Recent research shows that one minute of sustained laughter can be as effective as ten minutes of aerobic activity in releasing those endorphins which are conducive towards feelings of relaxation and contentment.

The following quote by the philosopher Gratzalin is apt:

> Everything done with laughter helps us to be human. It can be used to express an unending variety of emotions. It is based on guilt-free release of aggression, and any release perhaps makes us a little better and more capable of understanding one another, ourselves and life.

Conclusion

The need for students to develop their self-esteem has been the main theme of this book. The need for tutors to develop their own self-esteem together with their communication skills has been highlighted. It was argued that the enhancement of student self-esteem is dependent on the development of these skills in the tutor, as it is the quality of the tutor–student relationship that is the key to self-esteem advancement. Self-esteem enhancement exercises have been outlined as a supplement to this relationship, relying on the quality of the relationship for their effectiveness.

The final task for tutors is to communicate to their students that enhancing self-esteem is an active process and dependent on their own efforts. There will be no change without effort and their commitment to change. This means having to be prepared to face themselves and their problems. This can be an uncomfortable process, as it is always easier to go along with present inadequacies rather than make the effort to change. This is where the tutor's influence is paramount. Students need a tutor who can present to them a high self-esteem model and provide for them an accepting, trusting relationship. The rewards for both tutor and student will always be worth the effort.

Selected Bibliography

Argyle, M. (1996) *Psychology of Interpersonal Behaviour.* Harmondsworth, Penguin.

Bandura, A. (1977) *Social Learning Theory.* New Jersey, Prentice Hall.

Beck, A. T. (1989) *Cognitive Therapy and The Emotional Disorders.* Harmondsworth. Penguin.

Branden, N. (1995) *Six Pillars of Self-Esteem.* London, Bantam.

Burns, R. B. (1979) *The Self-concept.* London, Longman.

Burns, R. B. (1982) *Self-concept Development and Education.* London, Holt-Rhinehart.

Case, F. (1993) *How To Study: A Practical Guide.* Basingstoke, MacMillan.

Cattell, R. B. (1965) *Scientific Analysis of Personality.* Harmondsworth, Penguin.

Devine, T. G. (1981) *Teaching Study Skills: Guide for Teachers.* Boston, Alleyne and Bacon.

Ellis. A. (1993) *How to Stubbornly Refuse to Make Yourself Miserable about Anything.* Australia. MacMillan.

Eysenck, H. J. (1977) *Psychology is about People.* Harmondsworth, Penguin.

Fontana, D. (1989) *Managing Stress.* London. Routledge.

Gittins, R. (1985) *An Introduction to Literacy Teaching.* London, Albsu Publications.

Gilroy, D. E. (1995) Stress factors in the college student, in Miles, T. R. and Varma, V. P. (Eds.) *Dyslexia and Stress.* London, Whurr.

Gilroy, D. E. and Miles, T. R. (1996) *Dyslexia at College* (2nd Ed.) London, Routledge.

Gordon. T. (1974) *Teacher Effectiveness Training.* New York, Wyden.

Jung, C. G. (1921) *Psychological Types.* London, Routledge & Kegan Paul.

Lawrence, D. (1987) *Enhancing Self-esteem in the Classroom.* London, Paul Chapman.

Leader, D. (1990) *How To Pass Exams.* Cheltenham, Thorne.

McLoughlin, D. *et al.* (1994) *Adult Dyslexia.* London, Whurr.

Peelo, M. (1994) *Helping Students with Study Problems.* Buckingham, Open University.

Phares, E. J. (1976) *Locus of Control in Personality.* New Jersey, General Learning Press.

Priestley, P. and McGuire, J. (1983) *Learning to Help.* London, Tavistock.

Rogers, C. R. (1967) *On Becoming a Person.* London, Constable.

Thompson, M. and Watkins, B. (1990) *Dyslexia: A Teaching Handbook.* London, Whurr.

Williams, E. G. (1965) *Vocational Counselling.* New York, McGraw-Hill.

Index

acceptance, 42
affirmations, 88
anxiety, 39
assertiveness, 78
   exercises, 79
   using the right words, 80
assessing progress, 34

belittling & blaming, 22
body language, 75, 76
   exercises, 98

Cattell, 10
check list,
   communication skills, 50
   tutor skills, 53
compensation, 23
confidence, 4

defence mechanisms, 21
denial, 22
differences, 19
dimensions of personality, 13
dyslexia, 29

ego defense mechanisms, 21
ego-strength, 21
Ellis, 52
emotional deprivation, 15
emotionality, 14
empathy, 44
   exercise, 48
empowering the student, 61
expectancy effect, 63
experts, 98
extraverts, 10
Eysenck, 10

fun, 99

general learning difficulties, 40
genuiness,
   definition, 43
   exercise, 45
   goal setting, 97

hearing difficulties, 26
humour, 100

ideal self, 3
intelligence, 28
introvert, 10

Jung, 10

knowledge of results, 36

laughter, 100
learning,
   difficulties, 27
   objectives, 37
life events, 20
locus of control, 61

Maslow's Hierarchy, 5
materials, 73
meeting the student, 56
mind
   conditioning, 93
   structure, 93
modelling, 41
motivation, 35
   extrinsic, 36
   intrinsic, 36
motto, xi

nonverbal cues, 51

over-talkative student, 58

role play, 59

personality,
    factors, 38
    measurement, 12
physical deformity, 20
positive,
    feedback, 92
    lifestyle, 96

questionnaires,
    emotionality, 14, 70
    introversion/extraversion, 14, 71
    self-esteem, 68
    stress, 85

rational-emotive therapy, 52, 88
record keeping, 37
reducing feelings, 89
relaxation procedure, 86

self concept,
    acceptance, 74
    as motivator, 6
    definition, 1
self-esteem,
    definition, 4
    need, 5
    origins, 5
    programme, 67
    questionnaire, 68
self-image
    definition, 2

distorted, 18
strengthening, 91
skill development, 98
special needs,
    dyslexia, 29
    general learning, 27
    hearing, 26
    visual, 27
spontaneity, 73
student,
    empowering, 61
    personality, 9
    point of view, 63
    quiet, 56
    shy, 17
    talkative, 59
    temperament, 10
    understanding, 61
stress,
    minimising, 84
    questionnaire, 85
    relaxation procedure, 86

tutor,
    checklist, 53
    self-help, 52

unassertive behaviour, 16
unconscious mind, 93

visual,
    impairment, 27
    scotopic sensitivity, 27